How to Draw
Cool Stuff

A
Drawing
Guide for
Teachers
and
Students

Written and
Illustrated by

Catherine V. Holmes

LIBRARY TALES PUBLISHING

Published by:
Library Tales Publishing, Inc.
www.LibraryTalesPublishing.com
www.Facebook.com/LibraryTalesPublishing

For general information on our other products and services, please contact our Customer Care Department at 1-800-754-5016, or fax 917-463-0892. For technical support, please visit www.LibraryTalesPublishing.com

Library Tales Publishing also publishes its books in a variety of electronic formats. Every content that appears in print is available in electronic books.
Library of Congress Control Number: 2017944834

ISBN-13: 978-0615991429

PRINTED IN THE UNITED STATES OF AMERICA

How to Draw Cool Stuff

This is the one-stop-shop for creating beautiful and interesting artwork!

Inside you will find over 100 how-to, step-by-step drawings that are easy to follow and fun to do.

For Artists: Organized with chapters covering the elements of design, human face parts, perspective, holidays, animals, creatures, and more, "How to Draw Cool Stuff" presents hundreds of drawings demonstrating the images you can create just by combining simple shapes. Artists will learn to recognize the basic shapes within an object and turn them into detailed works of art in a few simple steps. These hands-on exercises will help you practice and perfect your skills so you can draw cool stuff of your own.

For Teachers: If you are on a limited budget, have limited time, limited resources, or have students that like to draw - this book is for you!

Inside you will find tons of lessons that are easy to transport and can be used to teach art to all levels of students. Each lesson includes easy-to-follow instructions where the whole process is viewed through a sequence of illustrations and minimal text. Also, each art project comes with a chart including the basic skills and concepts your students will learn along with final assessment tasks for your students to complete. The best part is - this is stuff that kids want to draw.

All you need is a pencil and paper and you are ready to draw cool stuff!

TABLE OF CONTENTS

Chapter 1
The Basics

Chapter 2
Human Face

Chapter 3
Perspective

Chapter 4
Holidays and Seasons

Chapter 5
Animals and Creatures

Chapter 6
Cool Stuff

About The Author

Catherine V. Holmes is a teacher, artist, youth advocate and author/illustrator of "How To Draw Cool Stuff."

"Art provides a venue for every person to learn.
I always tell my students, 'Everyone can draw,
but no one can draw just like you.'

Each individual brings their own style,
creativity and perspective to a work.
Look closely at an artwork and you can see
history, desire, fear or inspiration.
Through art, we have the opportunity for
creative problem solving
self-expression
artistic meditation and communication
an increased sense of personal well being
empowerment
relaxation
education
and a platform to showcase our personal
strengths in a meaningful way. This not only helps us
to become more perceptive in art,
but also in life."

INTRODUCTION

This book evolved out of necessity. After exploring art catalogs and libraries and wading through the "how to draw" section of book stores, I found a few good resources but none that had all the qualities I was looking for in a drawing book. Some ideas were too basic and often insulting to my older, more artistic students. Other material seemed to serve as a showcase for beautiful artwork but lacked any concrete instruction.

As a "travelling" art teacher with a limited budget and limited preparation time, I need a single resource that is easy to transport and can be used to teach all levels of students from middle school to high school and beyond. This book was created to fill that need and I want to share it with teachers and artists in similar situations. These projects will allow you to bring interesting and informative lessons that offer clear objectives and foster achievement without the need for expensive/multi-dimensional supplies: a regular pencil and eraser is all that is needed (sometimes a ruler or fine pen). Fancy art pencils, costly paper or kneaded erasers are not required for success. All pages have been student tested and approved.

The Book Details:

Inside you will find specific exercises that offer step-by-step guidelines for drawing a variety of subjects. Each lesson starts with an easy-to-draw shape that will become the basic structure of the drawing. From there, each step adds elements to that structure, allowing the artist to build on their creation and make a more detailed image.

Each art project comes with a chart including information that the artist should be able to **KNOW** (facts, basic skills), **UNDERSTAND** (big ideas, concepts, essential questions), and therefore be able to **DO** (final assessment, performance, measurements of objectives) by the end of the lesson.

This additional information gives these pages more power than just 'art for art's sake' - not that you need it - because art is important enough on its own! Artists are learning about themselves as expressive souls through the process of creating beautiful and interesting work.

The best part is, this is stuff that artists want to draw.

Information for Teachers using this Book:

Teachers can feel confident that they are using instructional time in ways that make a difference for their students when using this guide. Each lesson includes easy-to-follow instruction where the whole process is viewed through a sequence of detailed illustrations that can be linked to historical connections, your curriculum learning standards or adapted into an arts integration lesson. You decide how intense to make each project.

The projects can be differentiated to respond to students' diverse learning styles through a mixture of visuals and text.

For the best results, here are a few tips:

- Lessons are provided on mostly one-sided sheets for easy reproduction. Copy them on the photo setting of your school's copy machine if possible. The shaded areas will retain their best value.

- Post the "Know, Understand, Do" sheet provided on the board so students will clearly see the lesson objectives.

- Encourage your students not to skip any of the steps. Teachers may find that many students want instant gratification and often try to skip to the last step without following the process. There are a few art students who have a "talent" for drawing or have prior experience with drawing complex forms and do not need the steps, however, most do need to follow the sequence in order to achieve their best result. For greater success, they must follow the steps! By doing so, students are training their brains to see shapes within an object instead of the object as a whole. This will simplify the drawing process.

- Tell students to draw lightly. Once they have a basic outline and a few details, then students can make their lines darker and more permanent. Getting heavy-handed artists to draw lightly can be a constant battle but the struggle is worth it once they see the benefits. Erasing becomes easier and fewer papers are crumbled up and thrown away.

- Every student will find a different level of success with these drawing guides. Encourage students to make their work different from the exercises in the book by adding "extra's" and more details. This makes each work of art unique and personal.

- These simple steps can be adapted to any level - the student can put as much or as little effort into their work as their comfort level allows. NOTE: As a great art teacher, always push your students for more - going beyond the comfort zone is how we learn!

- The techniques and processes presented in this book are well within the reach of what your student can do. On occasion, some students may get frustrated and want to give up. Sometimes a student will declare defeat before even attempting the work. That is unacceptable! Remind them that creating art is a process. In cases like this, encourage your student to try just the first step. They will see that first step is quite easy and may be encouraged to try the next step, etc.

- If all of attempts at drawing seem to be preventing your student from achieving success, you may want to allow that student to trace. The drawings on these pages are presented on a smaller scale in order to discourage tracing, however, it is better to allow tracing as opposed to your student doing nothing at all. Modifications for assignments can include tracing if need be, just have the student add their own unique twist by shading or adding "extra's" that are not seen in the examples provided. Tracing without even trying - NOT OK!

- This book is great for substitutes. Copy a bunch of these lessons, put them in your sub folder and take your sick day without worry.

With enough practice, eventually students won't need a "how-to" book. A shift in the brain will occur and your students will be able to mentally break down the simpler image behind the complex one without assistance. That is when they will become Super Smart Artists!

Information for Artists using this Book:

Following these exercises is a great way to practice your craft and start seeing things in terms of simple shapes within a complex object. Professional art pencils and paper can offer a variety of results, however, the techniques discussed in this book can be successful by using everyday supplies.

This book is intuitive but you may come across a few challenging steps. Follow the tips below for best results.

- Try blocking out the information you don't need. When you begin drawing one of the artworks in this book, cover all of the steps shown with a blank piece of paper except for the first one. Draw just the first step that is exposed. After that step is finished, uncover the next step and work on it. By blocking out the steps you are not working on, the artwork becomes less challenging to attempt. Continue uncovering each step one by one and adding to your artwork until it is complete. It is a simple tactic but it works by getting you to focus on just one action at a time.

- Patience is necessary. Don't rush, take your time and practice patience. Don't crumble up your paper in frustration every time you make a mistake. Look at your artwork and figure out the lines that work and the lines that don't. Change them as needed.

This is easier when you:

- Draw lightly. Start with a light, sketchy outline and add more detail as the drawing progresses. Once all the lines look good to you, then they can be drawn darker and more permanent.

- Don't be too concerned with trying to make your drawing look just like the one in the book or spend a lot of time trying to get both sides of a supposed symmetrical object the same. Even our faces are not perfectly symmetrical. Your unique (and sometimes imperfect) approach is what will make the artwork engaging and beautiful. If your drawing doesn't look "perfect," that's OK!

- Want your artwork to look even more professional? Draw your object large then shrink it on the copier using the photo setting. The details and lines appear finer and your work looks more detailed. A great trick to try!

- Finally, don't worry about what your neighbor's artwork looks like. Remember: everyone can draw but no one can draw just like you. That is what makes art so special. If we all drew exactly the same way, art would be boring and there would be no point to it. Look at the way your art work comes out after you finish and compare it to your own previous work. You will probably be impressed with yourself!

Tips for Shading:

- "The Basics" chapter displays several different shading techniques. Using heavy pressure with your pencil will leave dark lines as light pressure will leave light marks. A combination of both with a gradual transition from one to the other is one approach to realistic shading. Practice using different pencil pressures to create a variety of tones.

- Be careful if you choose to smudge your artwork to create shading effects. The technique of smudging an artwork with a finger to create shadows can blur some intricately drawn lines and ruin a beautiful drawing. However, when done properly, smudging can be a quick and effective way to add depth to an artwork. This can be an acceptable practice, just beware of making mud! Rubbing too much will cause all of those fine lines and contrasting shades to become the same muddled, flat gray tone. This takes the depth away from a drawing and makes the work appear less detailed. For best results when shading with the finger rub technique, just smudge a little.

- You will see some examples in this book where hatching and cross-hatching are used. This is another shading technique which can be a unique alternative to smudging or pencil pressure when creating shading effects. Try them all and see which one works best for you.

Why We Need Art

Drawing makes you smarter! Believe it or not, artists are not just mindlessly copying what they see when following the activities in this book. By completing these projects, artists enhance their creativity and artistic confidence while gaining powerful tools for understanding what goes in to creating visual works. Students are actually re-training their brains to see in a different way. This allows them to express themselves and become competent, savvy, literate, imaginative, creative and perceptive in art and in life. Let your students, co-workers and the world know that ART IS IMPORTANT!

Chapter 1

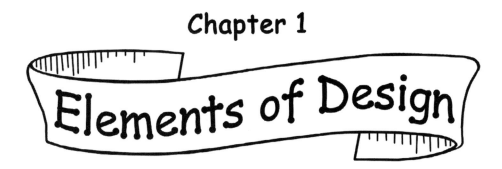

Elements of Design

ELEMENTS OF DESIGN

KNOW:
Elements of Design: color, value, line, shape, form, texture and space

UNDERSTAND:
• The basic components used by the artist when producing works of art
• How those components are utilized
• The difference between shape (length and width) and form (add depth)

DO:
Practice hatching, pointillism, texture, line, shape, form and space using a fine black pen in the space provided next to the examples on the handout. Copy what you see or create your own designs. Use the area in box number 7 to create an original design using at least 4 of the Elements of Design practiced in the boxes above.

EXTRA:
Create an original artwork on a separate piece of paper using at least 6 of the 7 Elements of Design. Fill the paper from edge to edge with your design.

VOCABULARY:
Elements of Design - Color, value, line, shape, form, texture, and space. The basic components used by the artist when producing art. The elements of art are the parts used to create subject matter in an artwork.

The Elements of Design
The basic components used by an artist when creating art
Color, Value, Line, Shape, Form, Texture and Space
Create examples of each in the spaces provided
Use a sharp pencil or fine black pen to complete the exercises below (we will skip color for now)

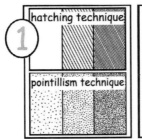

VALUE - the lightness or darkness of a color.
In this box you will show value using lines or dots.

TEXTURE - the way an object looks like it feels.
In this box, draw what you see or create your own texture.

LINE - a mark showing length and direction.
In this box, draw what you see or create your own line art.

SHAPE - an enclosed space showing length and width.
In this box, draw at least 4 different shapes.

FORM - an enclosed space showing height, width & depth.
In this box, draw the forms seen at left.

SPACE - distance or area between, around or within things.
In this box, draw the positive and negative space seen on left.

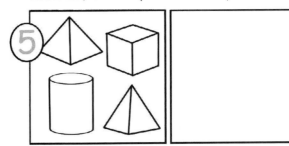

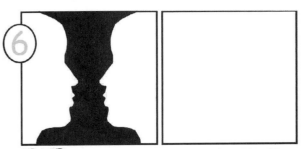

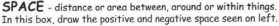

USE THIS AREA to create an original design using at least 4 of the Elements of Design practiced above.

21

SHADING SHAPES

KNOW:
Shading, Shadows and Blending Tones

UNDERSTAND:
• Value added to a shape (2D) when drawing creates form (3D)
• The lightness or darkness of a value indicates a light source on an object

DO:
• Recreate the 9 examples on the "Shading Shapes" handout, starting with creating a value scale
• Shade each object according to the value scale
• Blend values

VOCABULARY:
Blend - To merge tones applied to a surface so that there is no crisp line indicating beginning or end of one tone
Shading - Showing change from light to dark or dark to light in a picture
Shadow - A dark area cast by an object illuminated on the opposite side
Shade - A color to which black or white has been added to make it darker or lighter
Value - An element of art that refers to the lightness or darkness of a color

Shading Shapes

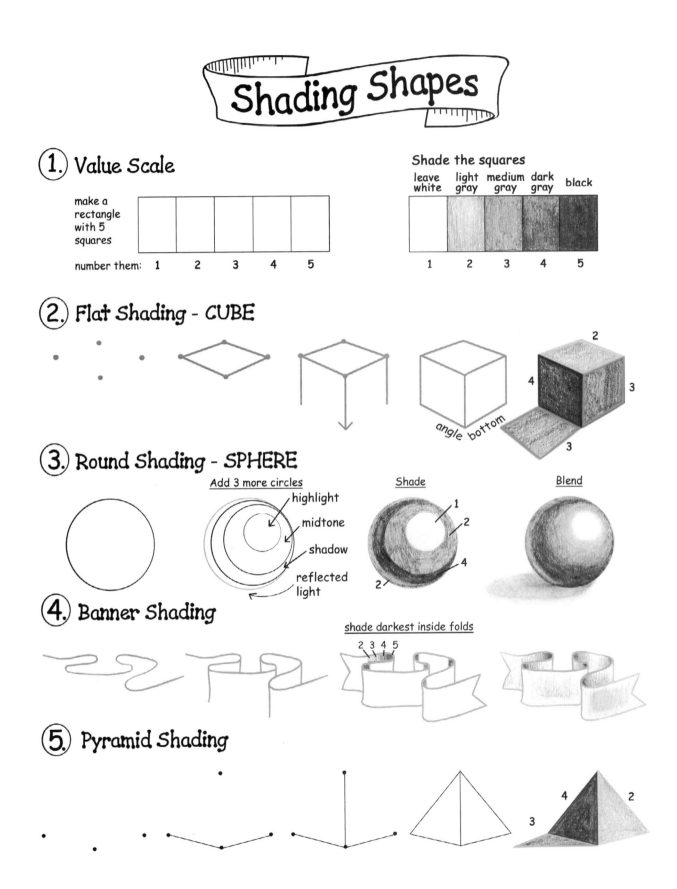

1. Value Scale

make a rectangle with 5 squares

number them: 1 2 3 4 5

Shade the squares

leave white	light gray	medium gray	dark gray	black
1	2	3	4	5

2. Flat Shading - CUBE

angle bottom

2

4   3

3

3. Round Shading - SPHERE

Add 3 more circles

highlight
midtone
shadow
reflected light

Shade

1
2
4
2

Blend

4. Banner Shading

shade darkest inside folds

2 3 4 5

5. Pyramid Shading

4   2

3

Shading Shapes 2

6. Coin

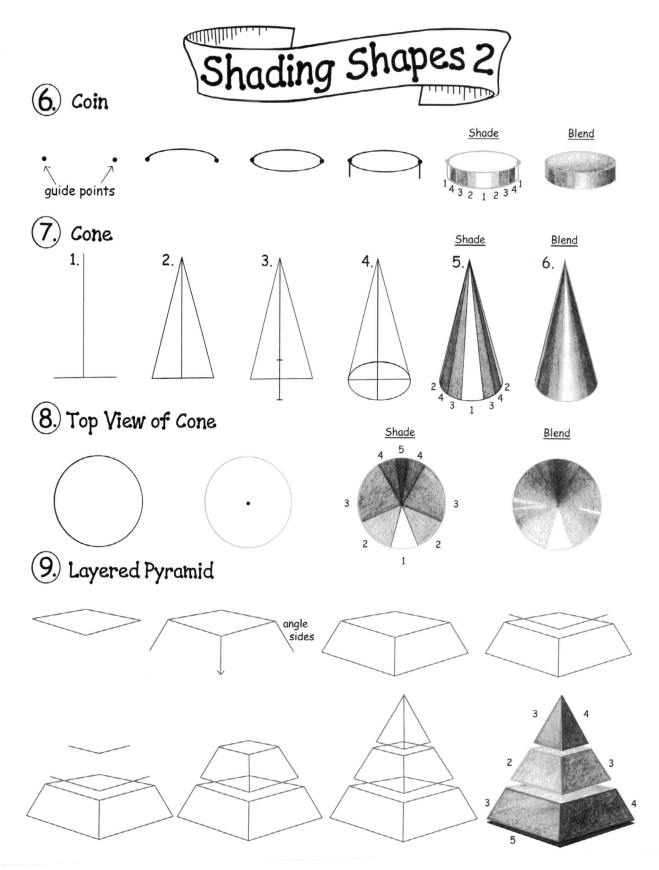

guide points

Shade   Blend

1 4 3 2 1 2 3 4 1

7. Cone

1. 2. 3. 4.

Shade 5.   Blend 6.

2 4 3 1 3 4 2

8. Top View of Cone

Shade   Blend

4 5 4
3   3
2   2
1

9. Layered Pyramid

angle sides

3   4
2   3
3   4
5

24

GETTING READY TO DRAW

KNOW:
Cross-Hatching, Hatching, Texture, Value Scale

UNDERSTAND:
- Texture is used by artists to show how something might feel or what it is made of
- Value added to a shape (2D) when drawing creates form (3D)
- The lightness or darkness of a value indicates a light source on an object

DO:
To practice different types of shading, complete the value scale, hatching and cross-hatching exercises in the area provided on the handout. On a separate piece of paper, draw a tree (or other object) that includes the types of shading practiced on the handout.

VOCABULARY:
Hatching - Creating tonal or shading effects with closely spaced parallel lines. When more such lines are placed at an angle across the first, it is called cross-hatching.
Shading - Showing change from light to dark or dark to light in a picture by darkening areas that would be shadowed and leaving other areas light
Texture - The surface quality or "feel" of an object; its smoothness
Value - An element of art that refers to the lightness or darkness of a color

Getting Ready to Draw

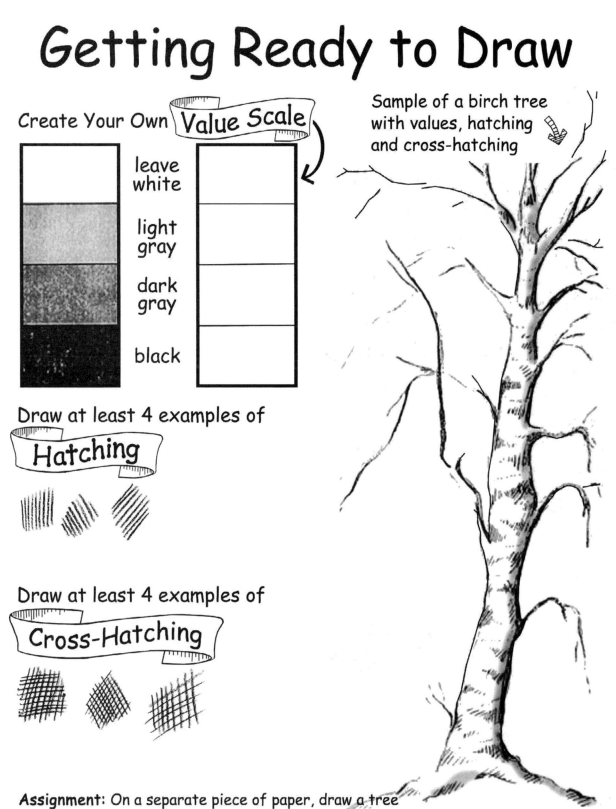

Create Your Own **Value Scale**

leave white

light gray

dark gray

black

Sample of a birch tree with values, hatching and cross-hatching

Draw at least 4 examples of

Hatching

Draw at least 4 examples of

Cross-Hatching

Assignment: On a separate piece of paper, draw a tree (or other object) that shows hatching, cross hatching and value scale.

LINE QUALITY (DOVE)

KNOW:
Lines are tools for communication

UNDERSTAND:
• Various types of line in an artwork add depth and interest, imply space, movement, light, and/or thickness (3D edge)
• Range in line quality heightens the descriptive potential in an artwork (textures, movement, light, space, etc.)

DO:
Create an original image using detailed line art that focuses on line quality. Experiment by drawing the artwork of the dove provided and add line weight in the contour areas highlighted on the worksheet. Next, try this technique on an item of your choosing, ensuring that some lines appear to come forward (thicker) and others recede (thinner).

VOCABULARY:
Line Quality (weight) - The unique character of a drawn line as it changes lightness/darkness, direction, curvature, or width; the thin and thick lines in an artwork that create the illusion of form and shadow

Line quality describes the appearance of a line - it's look, not it's direction (i.e. thick, thin, light, dark, solid, broken, etc.)

The olive branch and dove are symbols of peace

Introduction to Line Quality

Line Quality describes the appearance of a line (thick, thin, light, dark, solid, broken, etc)

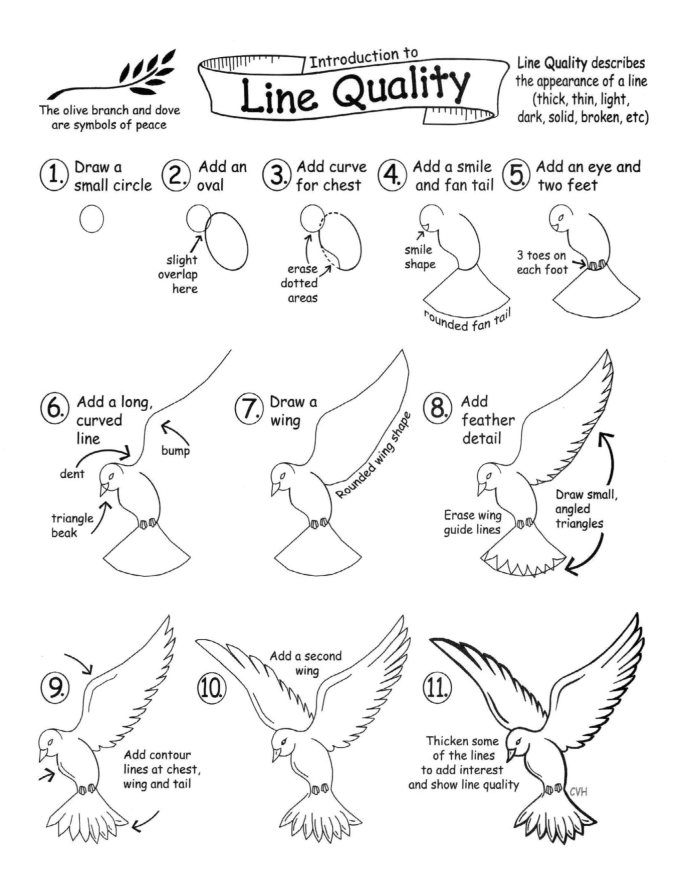

1. Draw a small circle

2. Add an oval
   slight overlap here

3. Add curve for chest
   erase dotted areas

4. Add a smile and fan tail
   smile shape
   rounded fan tail

5. Add an eye and two feet
   3 toes on each foot

6. Add a long, curved line
   bump
   dent
   triangle beak

7. Draw a wing
   Rounded wing shape

8. Add feather detail
   Erase wing guide lines
   Draw small, angled triangles

9. Add contour lines at chest, wing and tail

10. Add a second wing

11. Thicken some of the lines to add interest and show line quality
    CVH

These objects DO NOT HAVE...

Line Quality

...yet

Butterfly

Choose one of the following or create your own line drawing. **Add Line Quality.**

1.

2. Erase dotted areas. Add curves.

3. Add scalloped edges. Follow the contour of the wing edges to outline.

4. Draw "vein" lines

5. Add "Y" shapes to the vein lines

6. Add antenae and "tails". **Add line quality.**

CVH

Fishy

1. Start with 4 ovals

connect here

2. Add fin details

erase dotted areas

3. Add scales, eyes, & fin lines

CVH

Ginny's Mini

1. Start with 3 shapes

trapezoid

rectangle

upside down trapeziod

2. Add rounded detail

erase dotted areas

3. Add extra's

GINNY'S MINI

CVH

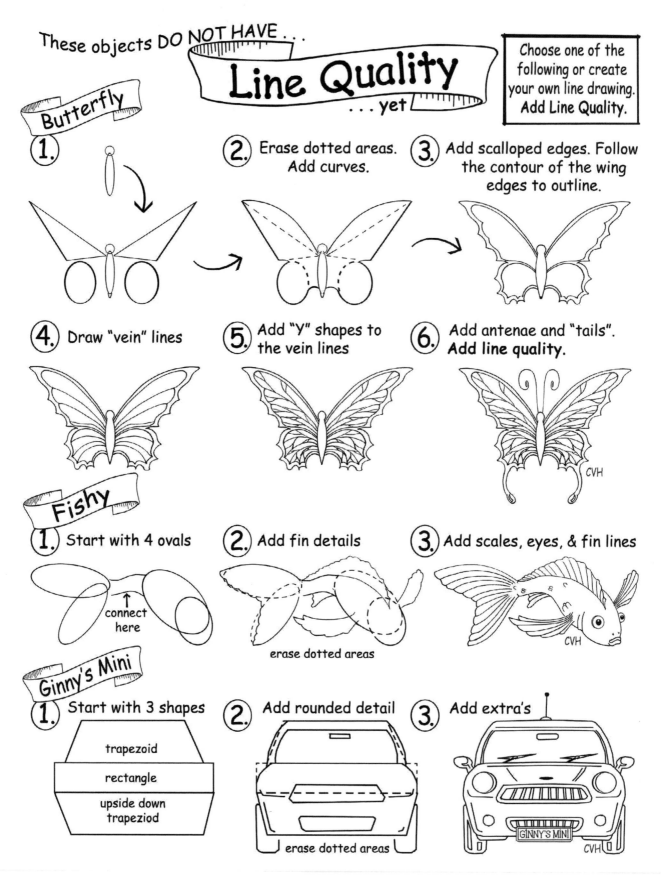

30

FORESHORTENING

KNOW:
• Simple steps to turn shapes into forms
• How to create the illusion of 3D

UNDERSTAND:
• Foreshortening is a way of representing an object so that it conveys the illusion of depth (3D)
• Foreshortening is when an object appears to thrust forward or go back into space

DO:
• Practice foreshortening by recreating the 7 mini drawings (5 on front and 2 on back) seen on the handout. Don't trace. Shade.
• Create an original drawing of a scene on a separate piece of paper that shows at least 5 examples of foreshortening

VOCABULARY:
Foreshortening - A way of representing an object so that it conveys the illusion of depth, seeming to thrust forward or go back into space

Foreshortening

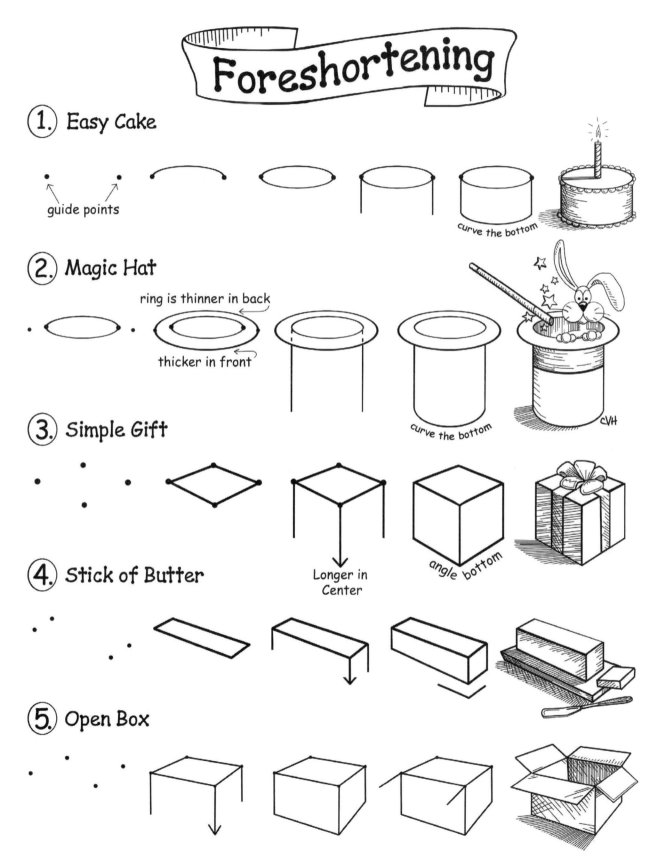

1. Easy Cake

guide points

curve the bottom

2. Magic Hat

ring is thinner in back

thicker in front

curve the bottom

3. Simple Gift

Longer in Center

angle bottom

4. Stick of Butter

5. Open Box

33

Foreshortening

(1.) Layer Cake

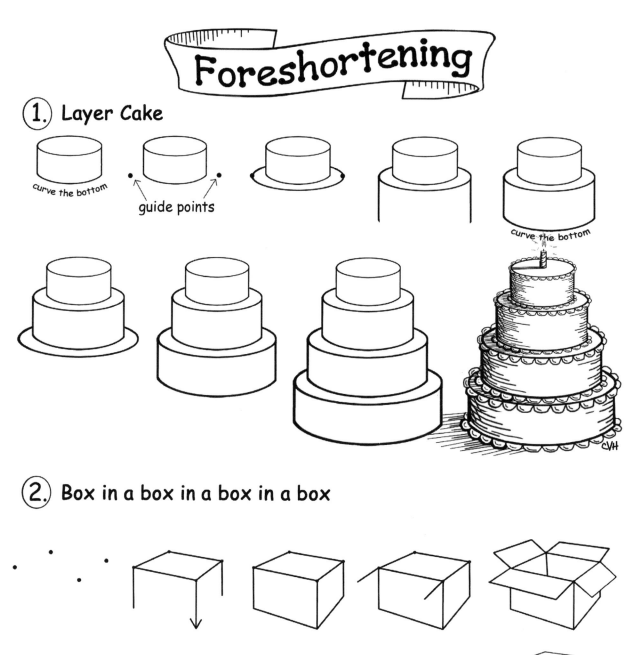

curve the bottom

guide points

curve the bottom

(2.) Box in a box in a box in a box

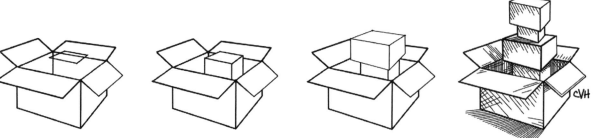

Question: I have 3 boxes. Inside those 3 boxes I have 3 boxes. Inside those 3 boxes I have 3 boxes. **How many boxes do I have?**

FORESHORTENED PERSON

KNOW:
Point of view

UNDERSTAND:
Perspective in which the sizes of near and far parts of a subject contrast greatly. Near parts are larger and farther parts are much smaller.

DO:
Practice foreshortening by creating a version of your own foreshortened person as viewed from above. Make sure the head of your character is much larger than the feet in order to give the appearance of foreshortening. Don't trace. Shade.

VOCABULARY:
Foreshortening - A way of representing an object so that it conveys the illusion of depth, seeming to thrust forward or go back into space. Foreshortening's success often depends upon a point of view or perspective in which the sizes of near and far parts of a subject contrast greatly.

Perspective - The technique artists use to project an illusion of the three-dimensional world onto a two-dimensional surface. Perspective helps to create a sense of depth or receding space.

Point of View - A position or angle from which something is observed or considered, and the direction of the viewer's gaze

Foreshortened Person

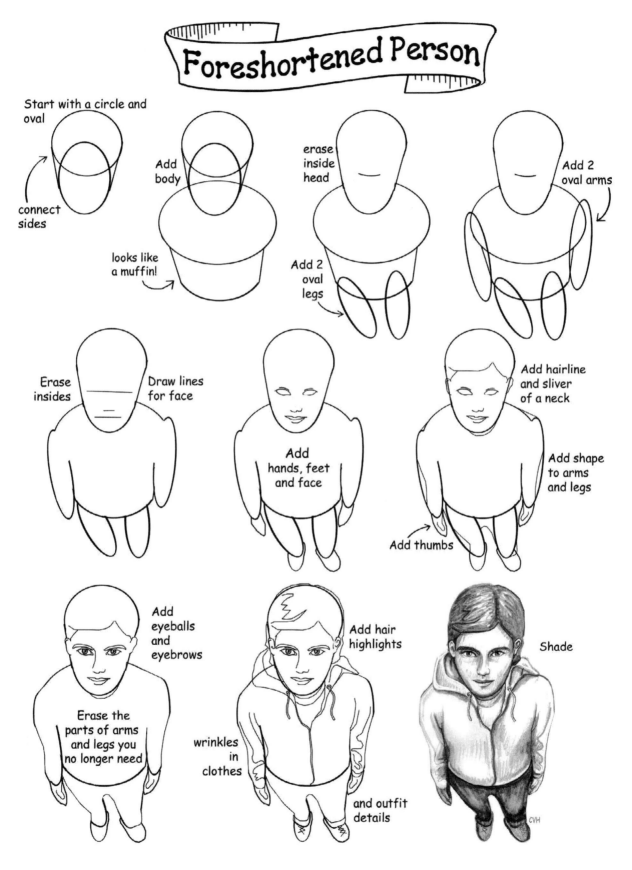

Start with a circle and oval

connect sides

Add body

looks like a muffin!

erase inside head

Add 2 oval legs

Add 2 oval arms

Erase insides

Draw lines for face

Add hands, feet and face

Add hairline and sliver of a neck

Add shape to arms and legs

Add thumbs

Add eyeballs and eyebrows

Erase the parts of arms and legs you no longer need

Add hair highlights

wrinkles in clothes

and outfit details

Shade

CVH

CONTOUR LINES AND TUBES

KNOW:
Contour lines surround and define the edges of an object

UNDERSTAND:
Adding lines to the inside of an outlined object give it shape and volume

DO:
• On a separate piece of paper, complete the 5 mini-drawings seen on the handout
• Draw your own original work focusing on the use of contour lines. Include: At least 5 bending tubes, 4 stacked round shapes, 3 cubes, 2 "furry" objects and 1 "extra".
• Don't forget Shadows!

VOCABULARY:
Contour - The outline and other visible edges of an object
Contour Lines - Lines that surround and define the edges of a subject giving it shape and volume
Tube - A hollow cylinder
Volume - The space within a form

Contour Lines and Tubes

Try all 5 drawings and the exercise at the bottom

A simple tube

$0 \rightarrow$ ... $\rightarrow$ ... $\rightarrow$ ...

1. Draw 4 tubes that bend

2. Draw a furry lollipop

3. Draw a fuzzy bear

4. Draw 4 stacked cubes

5. Draw 4 stacked ovals

EXERCISE:
Create your own contraption using tubes and contour lines

INCLUDE at least:
5 bending tubes
4 stacked ovals
3 cubes
2 "furry" objects
1 "extra"

BE CREATIVE!

INVENT

FIDO

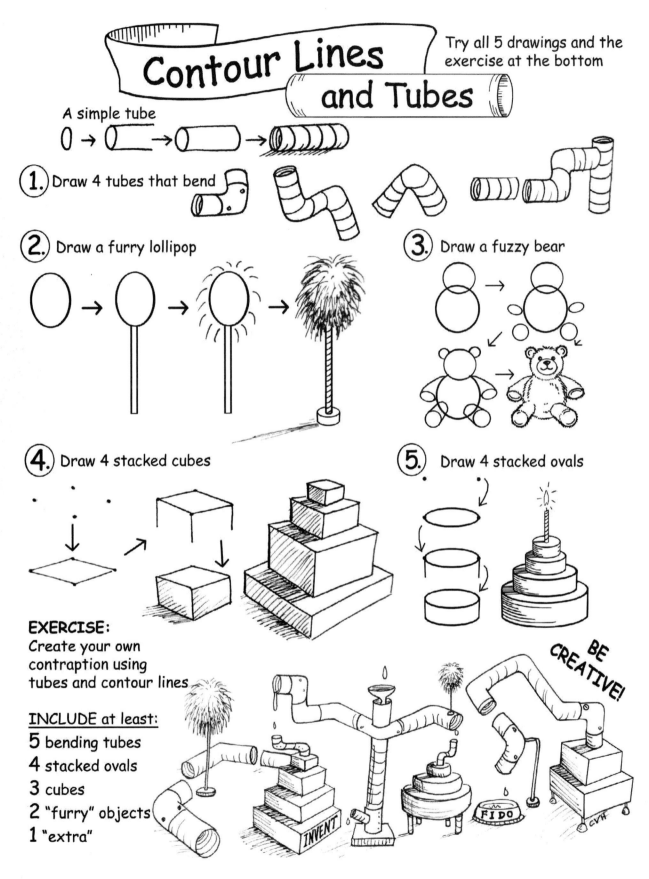

SHAPES TO FORMS

KNOW:
• Basic cylinder construction in drawing
• Shape and form are 2 of the 7 elements of art

UNDERSTAND:
• The difference between shape and form
• Volume

DO:
Look at the 2D images of shapes provided and use learned techniques to re-draw them as 3D forms

ASSIGNMENT:
Draw a glass of clear liquid with ice cubes and a straw. Don't forget - ice cubes float!

VOCABULARY:
Form - A three-dimensional shape (height, width, and depth) that encloses volume
Shape - An enclosed space
Volume - The space within a form

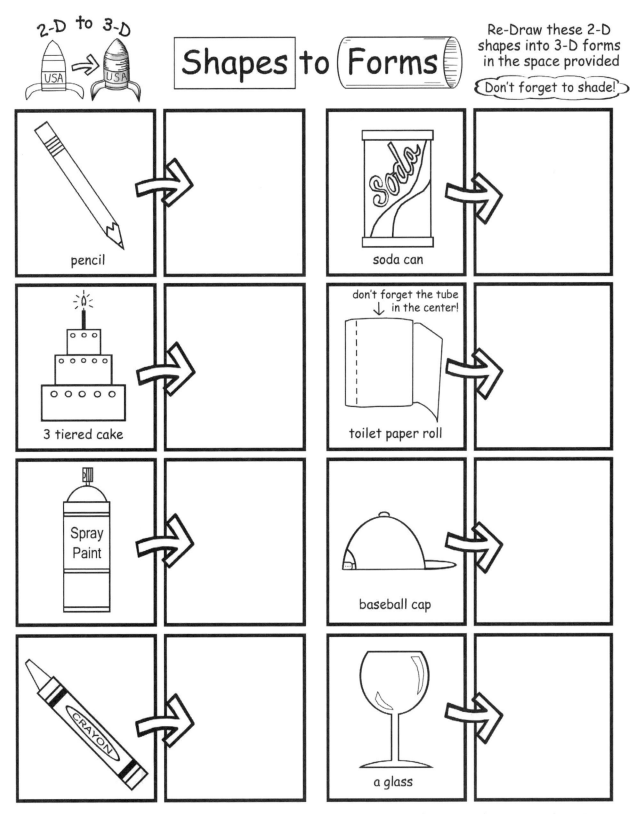

2-D to 3-D

Shapes to Forms

Re-Draw these 2-D shapes into 3-D forms in the space provided

Don't forget to shade!

pencil

soda can

3 tiered cake

don't forget the tube in the center!

toilet paper roll

Spray Paint

baseball cap

CRAYON

a glass

Assignment: On a seperate piece of paper, draw a glass of water with ice and a straw.
Remember: Ice cubes float!

CYLINDERS AND DISKS

KNOW:
Many objects (man made and natural) are based on the cylinder

UNDERSTAND:
• Cylinders in art give the appearance of a 3D circular tube
• Disks are short cylinders
• How to create the appearance of a 3D tube in a variety of objects

DO:
• Recreate the 7 mini-drawings in 3D as seen on the handout
• On a separate piece of paper, trace the outline of your hand and turn it into a series of segmented cylinders

VOCABULARY:
Cylinder - A tube that appears three-dimensional
Disk - The region in a plane bounded by a circle (also spelled disc)
Plane - A flat, two-dimensional surface

Practice Drawing Cylinders AND Disks

Draw the 3-D objects below

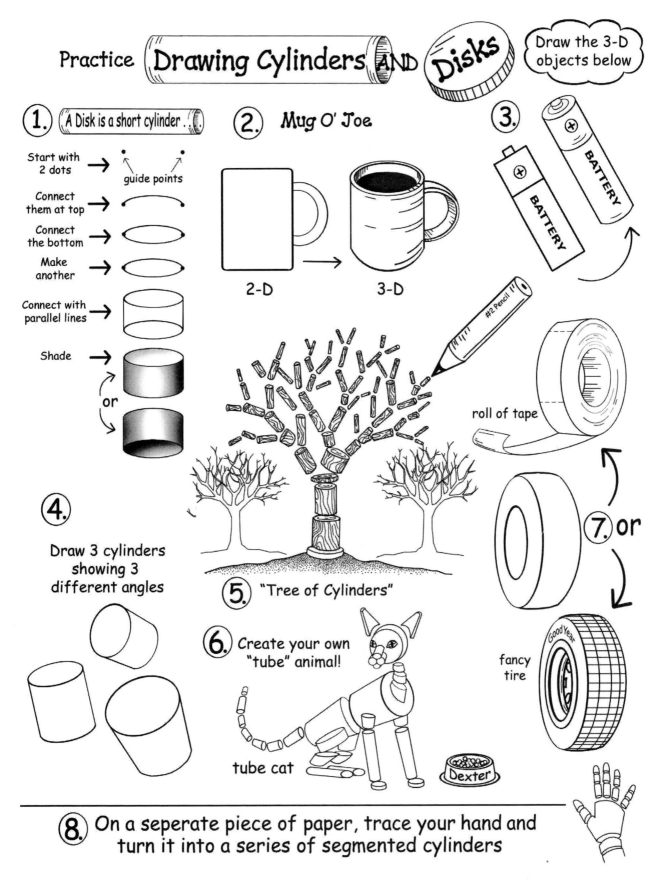

1. A Disk is a short cylinder.

Start with 2 dots → guide points

Connect them at top →

Connect the bottom →

Make another →

Connect with parallel lines →

Shade →

or

2. Mug O' Joe

2-D → 3-D

3. BATTERY BATTERY

#2 Pencil

roll of tape

7. or

fancy tire

GoodYear

4. Draw 3 cylinders showing 3 different angles

5. "Tree of Cylinders"

6. Create your own "tube" animal!

tube cat

Dexter

8. On a seperate piece of paper, trace your hand and turn it into a series of segmented cylinders

43

TIERED CAKE

KNOW:
Stacking and layering cylinders can create unique a structure

UNDERSTAND:
• Indicating both the top and bottom ellipse on a tube drawing (then erasing the area that is not seen) can aid in the creation of a proportionate cylinder

• Cylinders are one of the four basic forms that help an artwork appear three dimensional

DO:
• Start at the top of your paper and begin to practice creating short cylinders layered on top of one another

• Try and stack as many "cakes" as you can until the page is filled. Add different decorations for each layer to make it unique. Some ideas are candles, candies, swirly frosting, flowers, etc.

VOCABULARY:
Cylinder – A tube that appears three dimensional
Disk - The region in a plane bounded by a circle (Also spelled disc)
Ellipse – A circle viewed at an angle (drawn as an oval)
Layer – An item that lies over or under another item

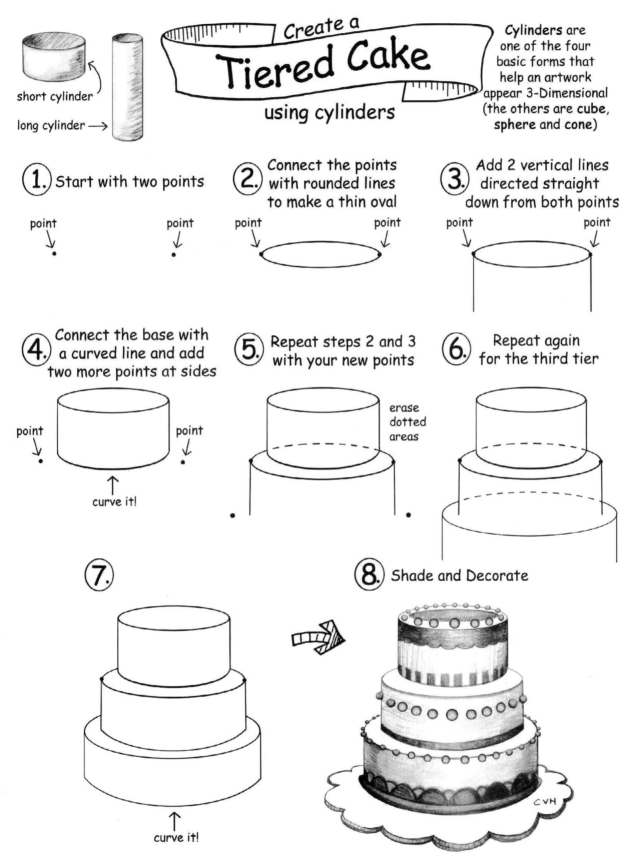

short cylinder

long cylinder →

Create a
Tiered Cake
using cylinders

Cylinders are one of the four basic forms that help an artwork appear 3-Dimensional (the others are cube, sphere and cone)

① Start with two points

point   point

② Connect the points with rounded lines to make a thin oval

point   point

③ Add 2 vertical lines directed straight down from both points

point   point

④ Connect the base with a curved line and add two more points at sides

point   point

curve it!

⑤ Repeat steps 2 and 3 with your new points

erase dotted areas

⑥ Repeat again for the third tier

⑦

curve it!

⑧ Shade and Decorate

CVH

45

PIECE OF CAKE

KNOW:
The techniques used to turn a shape into a form

UNDERSTAND:
• The difference between shape and form
• Parallel lines indicate direction as well as edges of an object
• Small additions can become major details when drawing objects realistically

DO:
Follow the steps provided to create a slice of cake in the form of a triangular prism. Add details, shading and "extra's" to create a unique artwork.

Note: "Extra's" are small details that the artist imagines and creates.

VOCABULARY:
Form - A three-dimensional shape (height, width, and depth) that encloses volume
Shape - An enclosed space
Triangular Prism - A three sided prism (polyhedron)
Volume - Refers to the space within a form

Piece of Cake

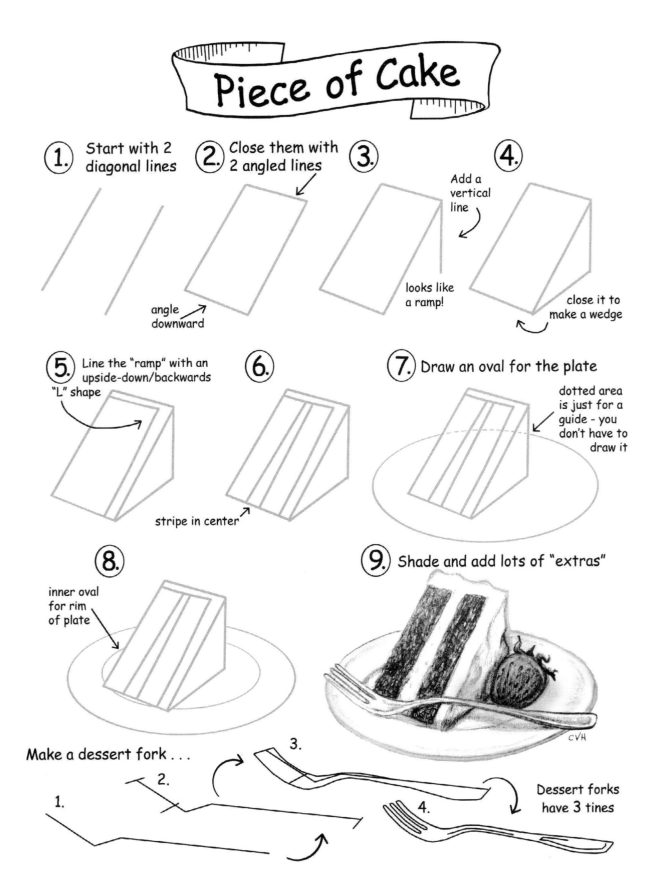

1. Start with 2 diagonal lines

angle downward

2. Close them with 2 angled lines

3. Add a vertical line

looks like a ramp!

4. close it to make a wedge

5. Line the "ramp" with an upside-down/backwards "L" shape

6. stripe in center

7. Draw an oval for the plate

dotted area is just for a guide - you don't have to draw it

8. inner oval for rim of plate

9. Shade and add lots of "extras"

CVH

Make a dessert fork . . .

1.   2.   3.   4.

Dessert forks have 3 tines

RIBBONS, SCROLLS AND BANNERS

KNOW:
Overlapping, Receding Lines

UNDERSTAND:
• Conveying an illusion of depth
• Varying sizes and placement on a receding plane
• Overlapping and shading gives the appearance of 3D

DO:
Practice overlapping and shading by creating your own Banner/Ribbon/Scroll using the provided techniques. Don't trace. Shade.

VOCABULARY:
Overlap - When one thing lies over or partly covers something else
Perspective - The technique artists use to project the illusion of 3D onto a 2D surface. Perspective helps to create a sense of depth or receding space.
Receding Line - Any line that appears to go back into space

Ribbons and Banners

1. Start with 2 slightly curved parallel lines

2. Add 4 angled vertical lines as seen below

3. Add the bottom edge of the ribbon

4. Close ribbon ends and add "cracks" for an aged appearance

   random "cracks"   torn edge

1. Start with one long, curvy line

2. Add a short vertical line coming down from each curved edge

3. Close the bottom of the ribbon with curved lines

4. Close both ribbon ends with a "〈" shape

5. Finish with words and shading

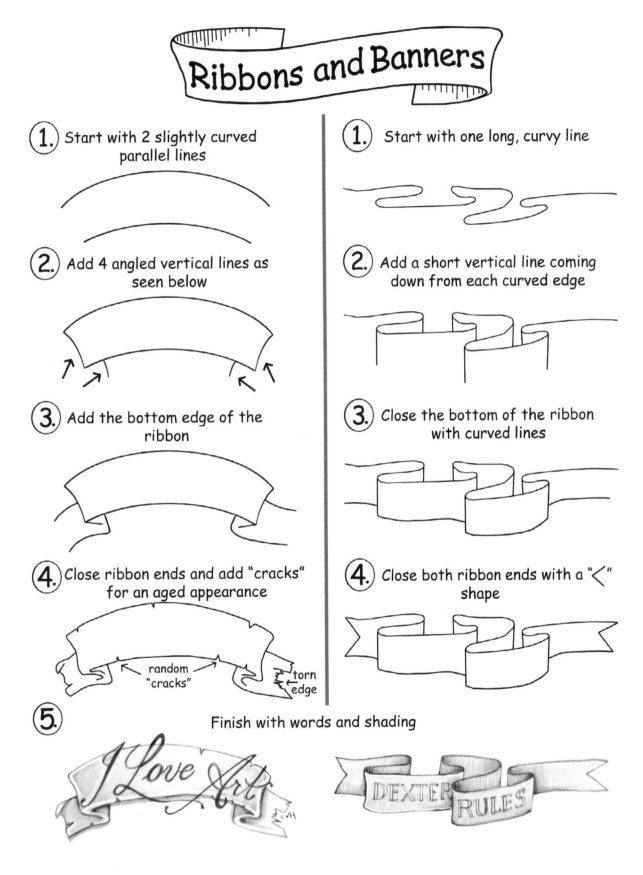

49

How to Draw Scrolls

1. Start with a curved line like this

2. Add swirls to each end

3. Add 4 vertical lines. These will be the ends of the scroll.

4. Connect tops with 3 rounded lines

Add 2 lines on each scroll to connect the curves

5. Shade

unroll the ancient Scrolls

Darker at edges where it curls

CVH

1. Start with a backwards "S"

2. Add swirls to each end

3. Add three horizontal lines

4. Connect swirls with vertical lines

Connect sides with rounded edges

5.

TREASURE MAP

CVH

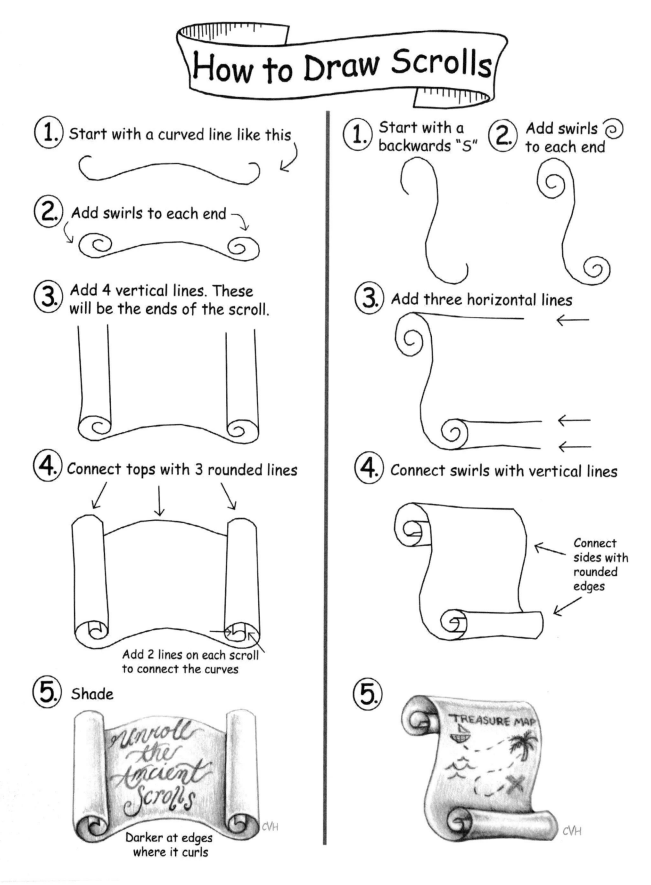

Rolling Scrolls

Double Roll

1. Start with 2 slightly curved parallel lines

2. Add 2 vertical lines at each end (closer at the center, wider at ends)

3. Add opposite facing swirls
‹ like this › as seen below
connect with curves

4. Shade darker at the overlapping/ folded areas

Single Roll

1. Start with 2 slightly curved parallel lines. The bottom is longer and "L" shaped
round edge

2. Create a mirror image of the vertical portion of the "L" shape
end banner with jagged edges →

3. Add swirl as seen below. Connect "rolled" portion with a round top
add "fold" details

4. Shade darker at folded areas

Opposite Roll

1.

2.

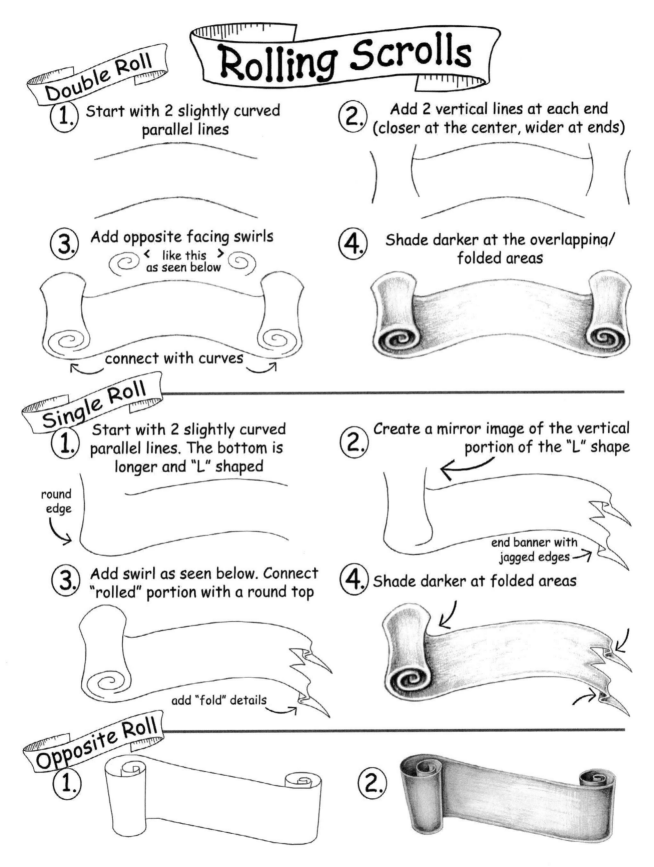

51

WAVING BANNERS

KNOW:
Curve, Overlapping, Perspective, Receding Lines

UNDERSTAND:
• Any 3D form (banner) can be created using a simple line as a guide
• Conveying an illusion of depth
• Overlapping and shading gives the appearance of 3D

DO:
• Draw your own Banner/Ribbon/Scroll using the provided techniques
• Add at least 2 folds to create dimension and interest
• Fill up the entire paper. Don't trace. Shade.

VOCABULARY:
Curve - A line or edge that deviates from straightness in a smooth, continuous way
Overlap - When one thing lies over or partly covers something else
Perspective - The technique artists use to project the illusion of 3D onto a 2D surface. Perspective helps to create a sense of depth or receding space.
Receding Line - Any line that appears to go back into space

Waving Banners

Start Here

1. Start with a backwards "S" shape
(Draw lightly as this line will eventually be erased)

2. Surround the top and bottom of the backwards "S" shape with lines

3. Add detail at the folds and ends

erase dotted areas

4. Shade and add text

WRAP AROUND LETTERING

Try Another

1. The backwards "S" shape is coiled loosley

2. Draw lines on both sides. Erase center

3. Finish ends

add a → "thickness"

show banner "folding" here

4. Shade and add a message

A Simple Banner

1. Draw 2 arching lines

2. Close each end with jagged lines

Catherine

Try adding text that extends beyond the banner

add random cracks to show age

More Waving Banners

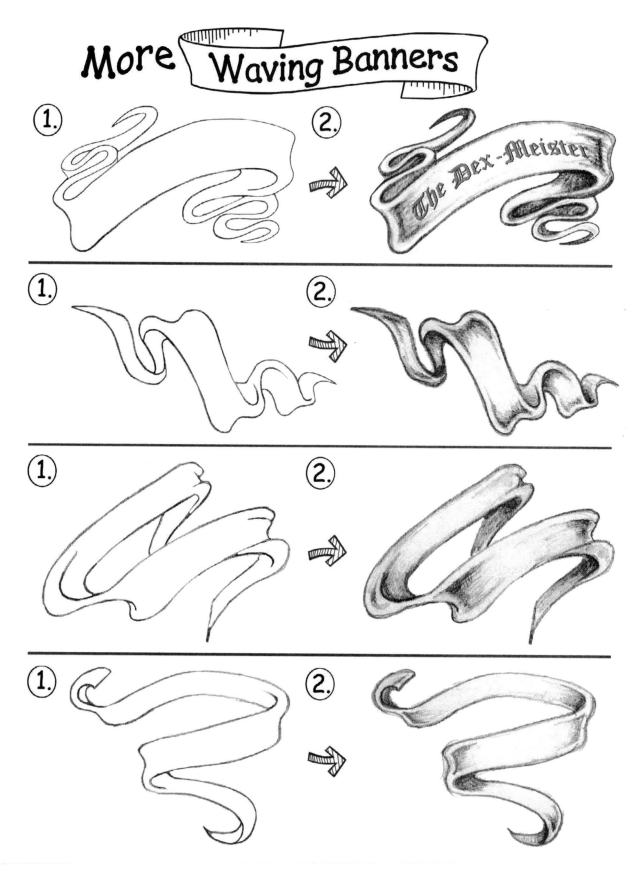

1.

2.

The Dex-Meister

AMERICA'S FLAG

KNOW:
A simple repetition of overlapping shapes can give the appearance of a waving flag

UNDERSTAND:
• Conveying an illusion of folds
• Wrapping stripes or patterns around the curves of a surface help to indicate realism and depth

DO:
• Create a waving version the U.S. flag using the tips and techniques provided
• Add 13 stripes to represent the original 13 colonies
• Add 50 stars to represent the 50 states
• Don't trace. Shade.

VOCABULARY:
Overlap - When one thing lies over or partly covers something else
Repetition - To draw the same shape again
Wrap - To draw over an object using contour lines to show form

America's Flag

1. Start with an angled rectangle

2 parallel lines
2 angled lines

2. Repeat the same shape as in step 1

slightly lower

3. Repeat again

even lower

4. Add 2 letter "V" shapes

5. erase dotted areas

Connect triangle to rectangle

6.

7. Round the points

round these 3

round these 4

8. Add stripes and area where stars will go

6 of the stripes shoule be below the star area

Add a total of 13 stripes to represent the original 13 colonies

9. Shade

blue

red
white

Add 50 white stars (or keep it simple and just add a bunch of white circles)

CVH

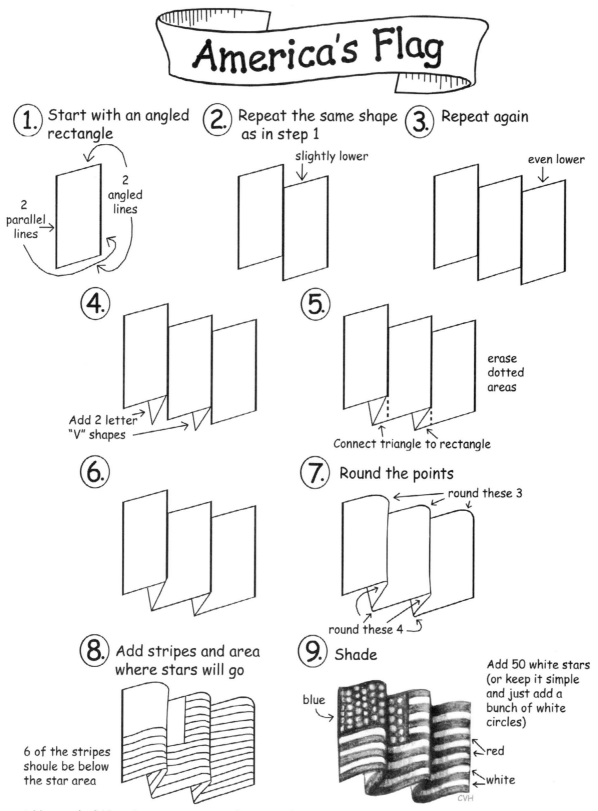

Chapter 2

Human Face Parts

THE HUMAN EYE

KNOW:
Visible parts of the eye (iris, pupil, sclera)

UNDERSTAND:
• The average human eye can be created by using standard guidelines/measurements
• The human eye is a sphere
• The average human eye is as wide as the distance between the eyes (one eye width apart)

DO:
• Practice drawing a basic human eye using the proposed techniques
• Draw lines that radiate out of the pupil (like spokes on a bicycle wheel) to indicate the many flecks of detail
• Add eyebrows and lashes last
• Shade. Erase a small area inside the iris for a highlight.

VOCABULARY:
Iris - Colored portion of the eye
Pupil - Darkest area of the eye, found in the center of the iris
Sclera - White part of the eyeball
Sphere - A three-dimensional ball shape, not a flat circle

Draw a Human Eye

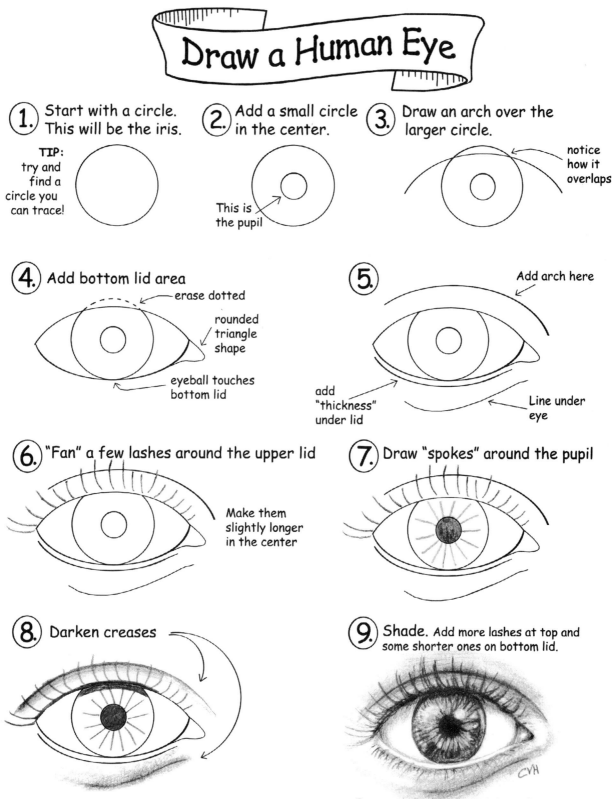

1. Start with a circle. This will be the iris.

TIP: try and find a circle you can trace!

2. Add a small circle in the center.

This is the pupil

3. Draw an arch over the larger circle.

notice how it overlaps

4. Add bottom lid area

erase dotted

rounded triangle shape

eyeball touches bottom lid

5.

Add arch here

add "thickness" under lid

Line under eye

6. "Fan" a few lashes around the upper lid

Make them slightly longer in the center

7. Draw "spokes" around the pupil

8. Darken creases

9. Shade. Add more lashes at top and some shorter ones on bottom lid.

CVH

Erase some spots in the iris to show shine. Add more spokes coming from pupil

EYEBALL

KNOW:
Iris, Pupil, Sclera, Sphere, Layering

UNDERSTAND:
• The difference between shape (length and width) and form (add depth)
• The use of proportion and observation to create a realistic eyeball
• Connecting a series of simple geometric shapes can create a complex (organic) object
• Layering and differences in the size of objects in a scene help to achieve the illusion of depth
• High contrast shading gives the appearance of form and 3D

DO:
• Follow the steps provided to create an original eyeball design focusing on balance, shading and blending tones
• Shade with pencil or colored pencil

VOCABULARY:
Iris - Colored portion of the eye
Pupil - Darkest area of the eye, found in the center of the iris
Sclera - White part of the eyeball

Eyeball

1. Start with a circle.

TIP: try and find a circle you can trace!

2. Add a small circle in the center. This will be the iris.

3. Add the last smaller circle in the center of the iris.

This is the pupil

4. Shade the pupil black. Draw "spokes" around the pupil.

5. Darken edges of iris. Add more "spokes".

Smudge/shade the outer eyeball rim to darken it

6. Shade entire iris. Add more spokes as needed.

Erase some areas on iris to indicate "shine"

Add a few thin lines for veins

CVH

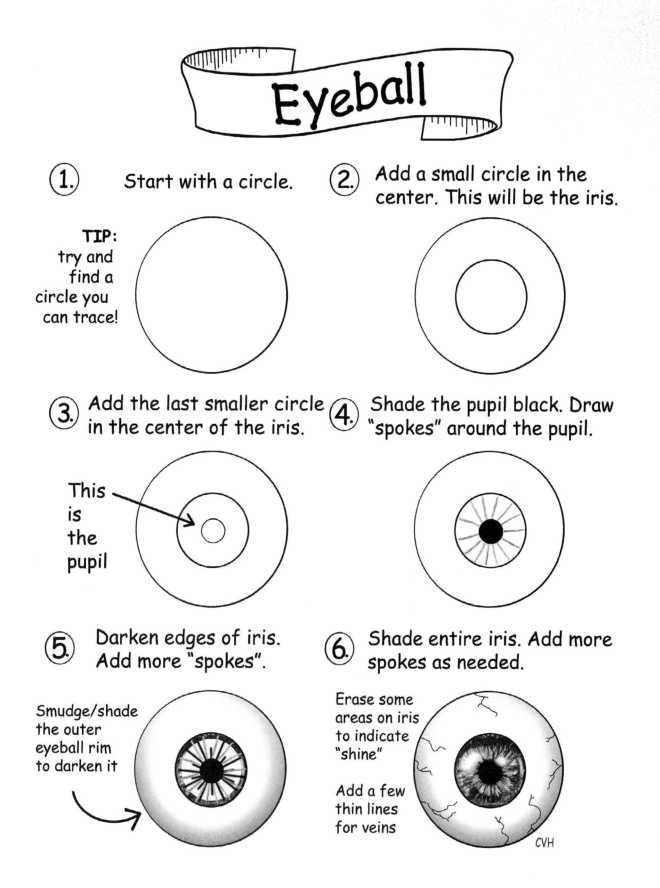

THE HUMAN NOSE

KNOW:
The average human nose can be created by using standard guidelines/measurements

UNDERSTAND:
• The average human nose is as wide as the distance between the eyes
• The nose protrudes and is usually lighter in the center and darker on the sides (depending on light source)
• A human nose is thin at the point between the eyes and gets wider as it moves down the face

DO:
Practice drawing a generic human nose using the proposed techniques. Shade with pencil and focus on shading, shadows and blending tones.

Tip: Don't make the nostrils too dark as they will draw attention from the rest of the face and look too "piggy"

VOCABULARY:
Shading - The blending of one value into another. Showing change from light to dark or dark to light in an artwork by darkening areas that would be shadowed and leaving other areas light. Shading is used to produce illusions of dimension and depth.

Draw a Human Nose

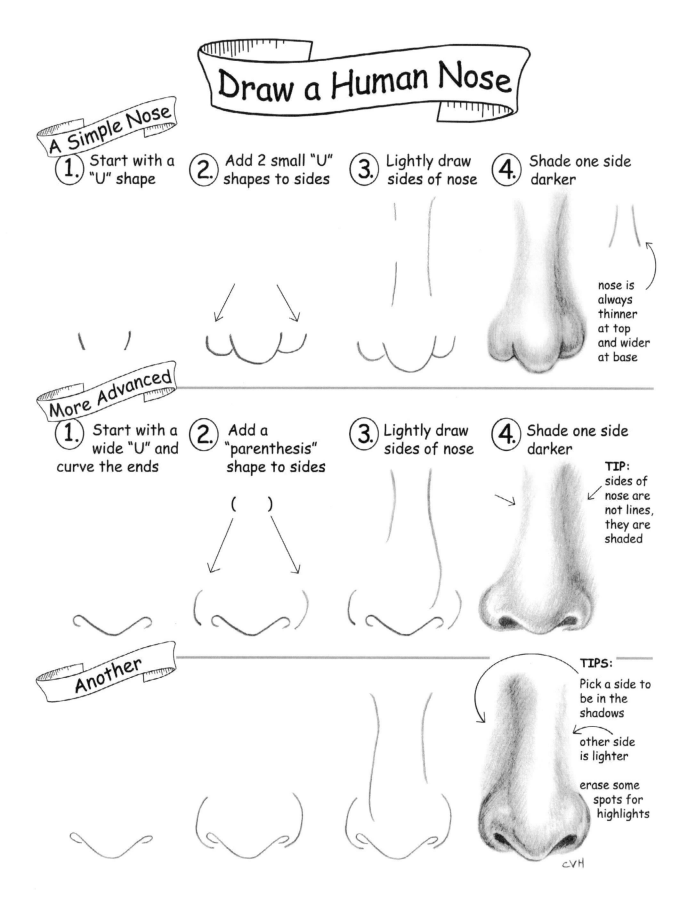

A Simple Nose

1. Start with a "U" shape
2. Add 2 small "U" shapes to sides
3. Lightly draw sides of nose
4. Shade one side darker

nose is always thinner at top and wider at base

More Advanced

1. Start with a wide "U" and curve the ends
2. Add a "parenthesis" shape to sides
3. Lightly draw sides of nose
4. Shade one side darker

TIP: sides of nose are not lines, they are shaded

Another

TIPS:
Pick a side to be in the shadows

other side is lighter

erase some spots for highlights

cVH

Pick a Nose

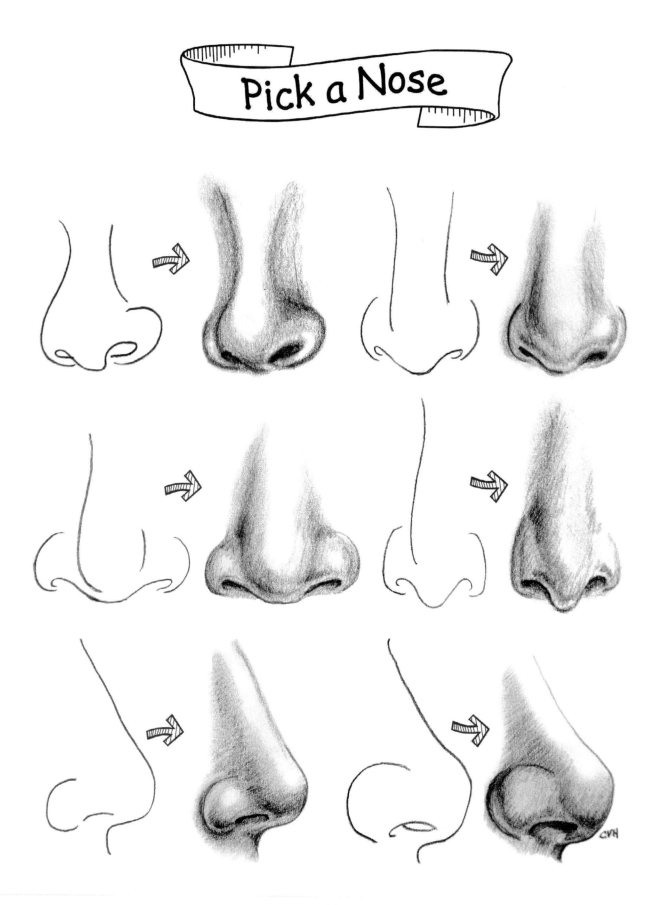

THE HUMAN MOUTH

KNOW:
The average human mouth can be drawn realistically by using standard guidelines/ measurements. (When drawing a face, measure from the pupils downward for width).

UNDERSTAND:
• The average human bottom lip is fuller and larger than the top lip (on most people!)
• Shading in the direction of the planes of the lip create form, curved lines create contour

DO:
• Practice drawing a basic human mouth using the proposed techniques
• Shade
• Make the darkest value on the line where the lips meet. Erase some spots in the center bottom lip to create a natural shine effect.

Draw a Human Mouth

1. Start with a "sunset" shape

2. Make rounded indent at center

erase dotted area

3. Make 2 more rounded indents (this time at bottom)

erase dotted areas

4. Add a short line to indicate the location of the bottom lip

MOST people have a bigger bottom lip than upper

5. Connect the bottom lip with curving lines

6. Add lip lines

curved lines to show lip contour

smile lines

shadow line

7. Shade

TIP:

Don't try to make both sides perfect. Human faces are not exactly symmetrical!

erase some areas on center bottom lip for highlights

CVH

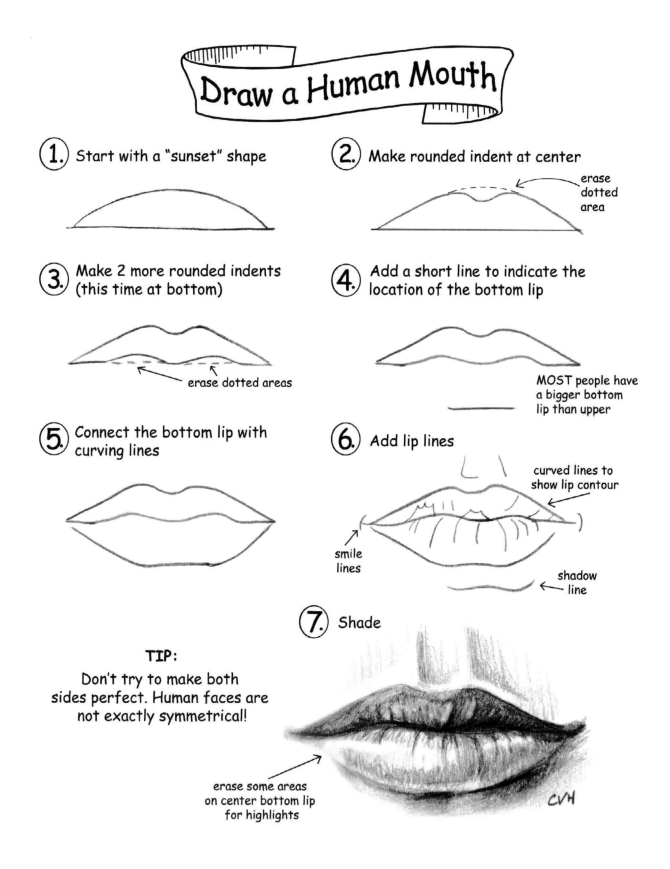

THE HUMAN EAR

KNOW:
• The ear is the organ of the human body that detects sound and aids in balance and body position
• Human ears are placed somewhat symmetrically on opposite sides of the head

UNDERSTAND:
• The average human ear can be drawn realistically by using standard guidelines/ measurements (measure from the edge of the eye line to the bottom of the nose line when drawing ears on a head)
• Shading using value scale tones will achieve a more realistic rendering

DO:
• Practice drawing a basic human ear using the proposed techniques
• Make the darkest value inside the "circle" and under the top rounded area. Erase some spots on the lobe to create a natural shine effect.

VOCABULARY:
Symmetry - The same on both sides; balanced proportions

Draw a Human Ear

1. Start with 2 overlapping circles on a diagonal

larger circle →

smaller circle →

2. Erase parts shown with dash lines

connect with a line here ↖

3. Draw the top of a question mark shape

"?" without the bottom dot →

4. Add a small circle

5. Add more as seen below . . .

Add a small triangle →

another curved line →

6. Add a few more details

Add 2 more lines here ⤵

curve this line upward and inward →

7. Make these 2 shapes and shade them in

8. Fill in the areas as seen below

9. Shade

CVH

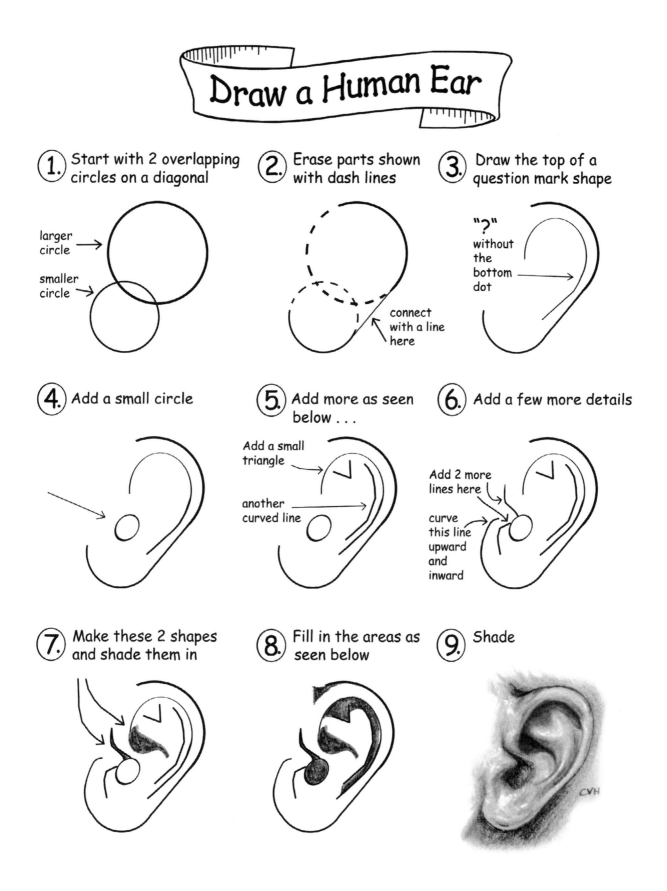

THE HUMAN HEAD

KNOW:
The simple steps to create a human face

UNDERSTAND:
• The use of proportion to create a head and generic features
• Subtle difference in the shape and size of specific features make us look unique
• Protruding objects (nose, lips, etc.) create shadows
• The human head can be measured/created on a grid

DO:
• Practice drawing a generic human face/head using the proposed techniques
• Start with guide lines, place the features, shade
• Follow the "Face Checklist"

LATER . . .
Self Portraits - Start with a basic face grid then use a mirror to see the shape and size of your individual features. Focus on identity and individuality - it's those small deviations from a generic face that make us look unique!

VOCABULARY:
Proportion - The comparative sizes and placement of one part to another

FACE CHECKLIST

HEAD:
Shade under brows, neck, nose, lower lip, chin, and possibly cheekbones (depending on light source)

LIPS:
• On most people, the upper lip is smaller (and shaded in slightly darker) than the lower
• Erase a spot in the lower lip for a "shine"
• Draw rounded, contour lines to indicate form

EYES:
• Color the pupil black, the iris lighter
• Draw "spokes" radiating from pupil for detail
• Leave a white highlight somewhere in the iris
• Upper part of the eye (lash line) should be darker than the lower
• Lashes are shorter as they grow towards the center of face

NOSE:
• Side of nose shaded (not outlined)
• Watch out for the "piggy" nose

LAST , BUT NOT LEAST . . .
• Erase guidelines
• Create eyebrows, lashes and a hair style

NOTE: Hair is usually shaded darker than the skin on most people. The darkest shading on your paper should be: hair, eyeballs (iris/pupils) and eye brows. This is for most faces but there are a few exceptions.

TIP: When drawing your own face, hold mirror directly in front of you. Some students look down at the mirror and get a view straight up their noses! This makes for an unflattering self-portrait.

A Basic Human Face

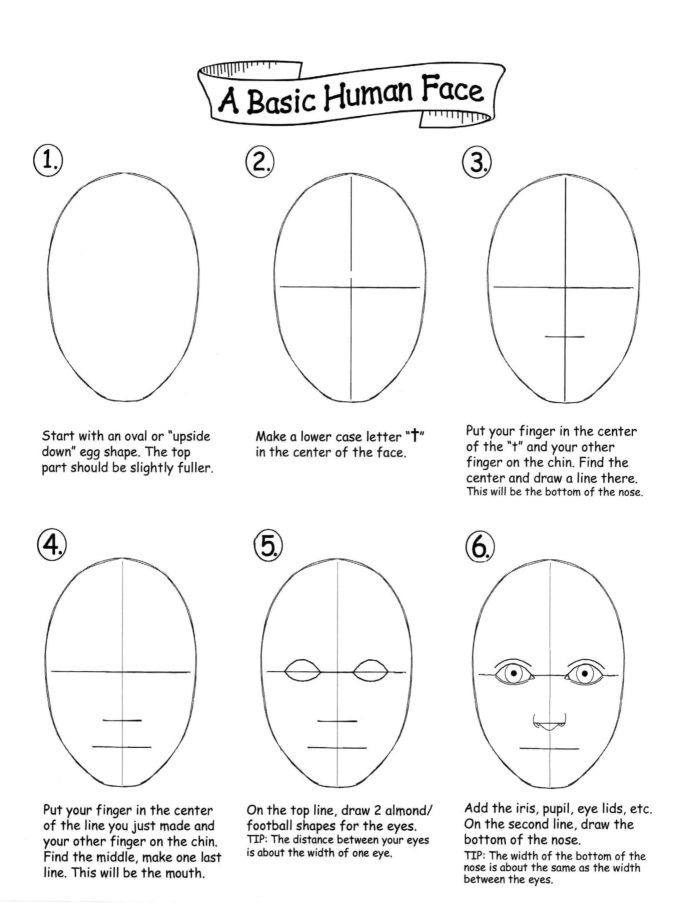

(1.) Start with an oval or "upside down" egg shape. The top part should be slightly fuller.

(2.) Make a lower case letter "t" in the center of the face.

(3.) Put your finger in the center of the "t" and your other finger on the chin. Find the center and draw a line there. This will be the bottom of the nose.

(4.) Put your finger in the center of the line you just made and your other finger on the chin. Find the middle, make one last line. This will be the mouth.

(5.) On the top line, draw 2 almond/ football shapes for the eyes.
TIP: The distance between your eyes is about the width of one eye.

(6.) Add the iris, pupil, eye lids, etc. On the second line, draw the bottom of the nose.
TIP: The width of the bottom of the nose is about the same as the width between the eyes.

A Basic Human Face

... continued

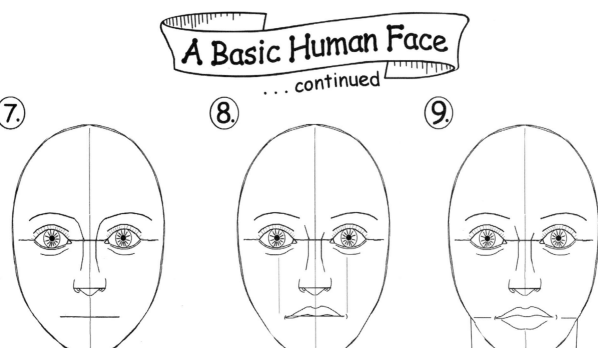

7.

Add "spokes" in the iris and lines for the brows and sides of the nose. TIP #1: The sides of your nose are connected to your brows! TIP #2: The fattest part of the nose is the base, the thinnest part is between the brows. (think triangle shaped)

8.

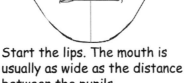

Start the lips. The mouth is usually as wide as the distance between the pupils.

TIP: Don't forget to add the "Cupid's Bow": the little divit at the top of the upper lip.

9.

Add the neck lines.
TIP: The neck is about as wide as the edges of the mouth lines.
Add the bottom lip.
TIP: The bottom is usually fuller than the upper on MOST people.

10

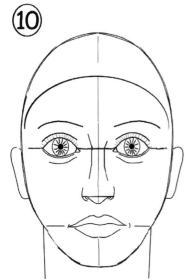

Add the hairline (looks like a swim cap). Add the ears.
TIP: The top of the ear lines up with the eye line, the bottom of the ear lines up with the bottom of the nose.

11

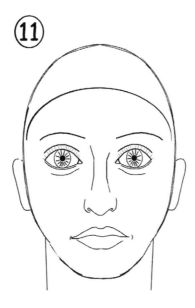

Erase the guide lines.

12

CVH

Add hair and shade.

THE HUMAN SKULL

KNOW:
• Simple steps to create a human skull
• Major bones of the head

UNDERSTAND:
• The basics of proportion to create a skull
• Features of the human head can be measured/created on a grid

DO:
• Practice drawing a generic human face/head using the proposed techniques
• Start with guide lines, place the features, shade

VOCABULARY:
Cranium - Portion of the skull that encloses the braincase
Human Skull - Supports the structures of the face and forms a cavity for the brain
Mandible - The lower jawbone
Proportion - The comparative sizes and placement of one part to another

Draw a Human Skull

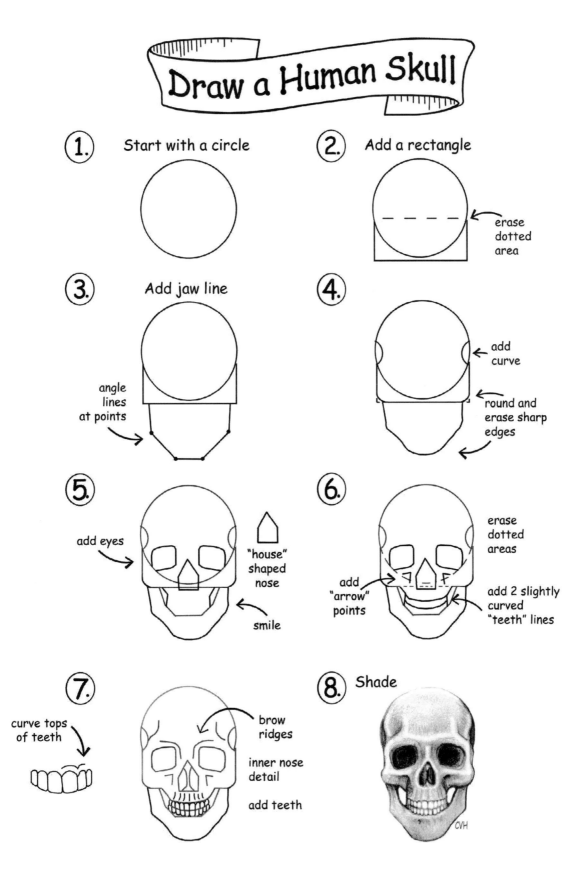

1. Start with a circle

2. Add a rectangle
erase dotted area

3. Add jaw line
angle lines at points

4.
add curve
round and erase sharp edges

5.
add eyes
"house" shaped nose
smile

6.
erase dotted areas
add "arrow" points
add 2 slightly curved "teeth" lines

7.
curve tops of teeth

brow ridges
inner nose detail
add teeth

8. Shade

CVH

Chapter 3

Perspective

ONE POINT PERSPECTIVE

KNOW:
One Point Perspective

UNDERSTAND:
• In linear perspective, all lines appear to meet at a **single** point on the horizon
• Receding lines create straight edges that appear to go back into space

DO:
• Create an original artwork of a street scene using a horizon line, vanishing point, and receding lines to indicate the illusion of 3D

INCLUDE:
• At least 6 buildings
• A road
• Details like windows, bricks, and doorways
• "Extras" like a car, street signs or billboards

VOCABULARY:
Horizon Line - A line where water or land appears to end and the sky begins
One Point Perspective - A form of linear perspective in which all lines appear to meet at a single point on the horizon
Receding Lines - Lines that move back or away from the foreground
Vanishing Point - A point on a horizon line where lines between near and distant objects appear to meet in order to produce an illusion of depth

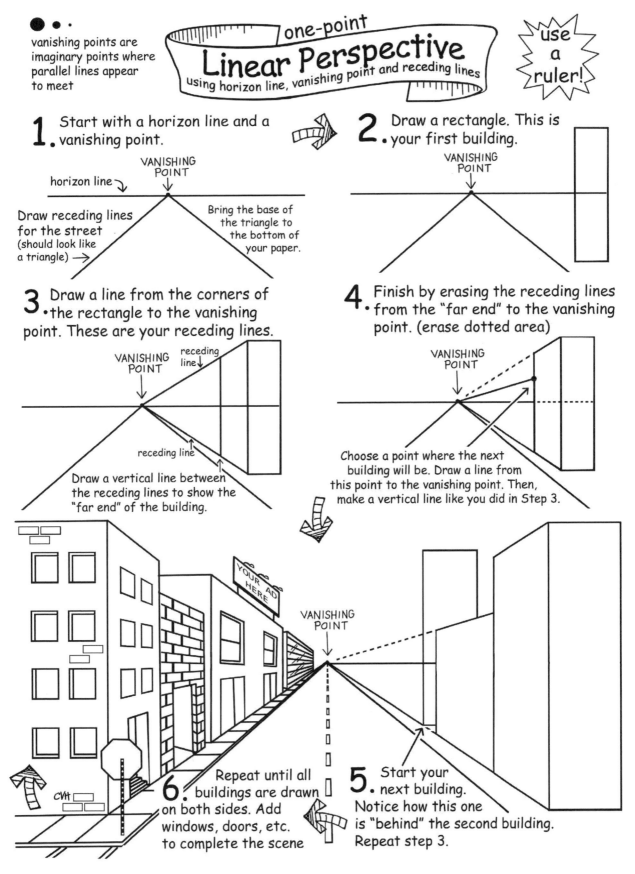

vanishing points are imaginary points where parallel lines appear to meet

one-point Linear Perspective
using horizon line, vanishing point and receding lines

use a ruler!

1. Start with a horizon line and a vanishing point.

VANISHING POINT

horizon line

Draw receding lines for the street (should look like a triangle) →

Bring the base of the triangle to the bottom of your paper.

2. Draw a rectangle. This is your first building.

VANISHING POINT

3. Draw a line from the corners of the rectangle to the vanishing point. These are your receding lines.

VANISHING POINT

receding line

receding line

Draw a vertical line between the receding lines to show the "far end" of the building.

4. Finish by erasing the receding lines from the "far end" to the vanishing point. (erase dotted area)

VANISHING POINT

Choose a point where the next building will be. Draw a line from this point to the vanishing point. Then, make a vertical line like you did in Step 3.

YOUR AD HERE

VANISHING POINT

CVH

6. Repeat until all buildings are drawn on both sides. Add windows, doors, etc. to complete the scene

5. Start your next building. Notice how this one is "behind" the second building. Repeat step 3.

TWO POINT PERSPECTIVE

KNOW:
Two Point Perspective

UNDERSTAND:
• In linear perspective, all lines appear to meet at either of **two** points on the horizon
• Techniques of perspective are used to create the illusion of depth
• Variation between sizes of subjects
• Overlapping
• Placing objects on the depicted ground as lower when nearer and higher on the page when farther away

DO:
Create an original artwork of a street scene using a horizon line, **2** vanishing points, and receding lines to indicate the illusion of 3D

INCLUDE:
At least 7 buildings, 2 roads, details like windows, bricks, and doorways, and lots of "extra's"

VOCABULARY:
Depth - The distance from front to back or near to far in an artwork
Two Point Perspective - A form of linear perspective in which all lines appear to meet at one of two points on the horizon

The buildings you are drawing may fall below or rise above the horizon line.

two-point
Linear Perspective
using horizon line, vanishing point and receding lines

use a ruler!

1. Start with a horizon line and TWO vanishing points and a vertical line for your first building.

VANISHING POINT

VANISHING POINT

2. Next, draw receding lines from your center vertical line to BOTH vanishing points.

VANISHING POINT

VANISHING POINT

3. Draw 2 more lines on either side of the center vertical line. This will be your first building.

VANISHING POINT

VANISHING POINT

4. Create another, smaller building. Notice that this new buildings' top is BELOW the horizon line.

use a receding and a vertical line

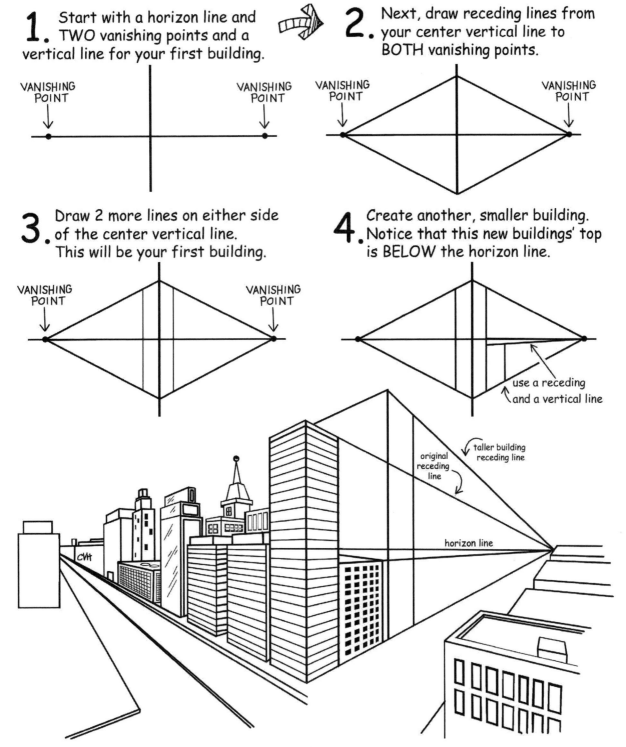

taller building receding line

original receding line

horizon line

CV/t

83

AERIAL VIEWPOINT

KNOW:
Aerial Viewpoint

UNDERSTAND:
• Techniques used to create a "birds-eye" view
• Use of receding lines

DO:
• Create an original "bird's eye" view of a city scene using a vanishing point and receding lines

INCLUDE:
• At least 8 buildings
• Details like windows, bricks, and doorways
• Trees, roads, and other "extras" around the base of buildings
• Rooftop Details: Fans, pools, vents, helicopter pads and other things you would find on a rooftop

VOCABULARY:
Aerial Viewpoint - Seeing from a point of view at a great height, also called a bird's-eye view

Bird's-Eye View - An elevated view of an object from above, with a perspective as though the observer were a bird. This technique is often used in the making of blueprints, floor plans and maps.

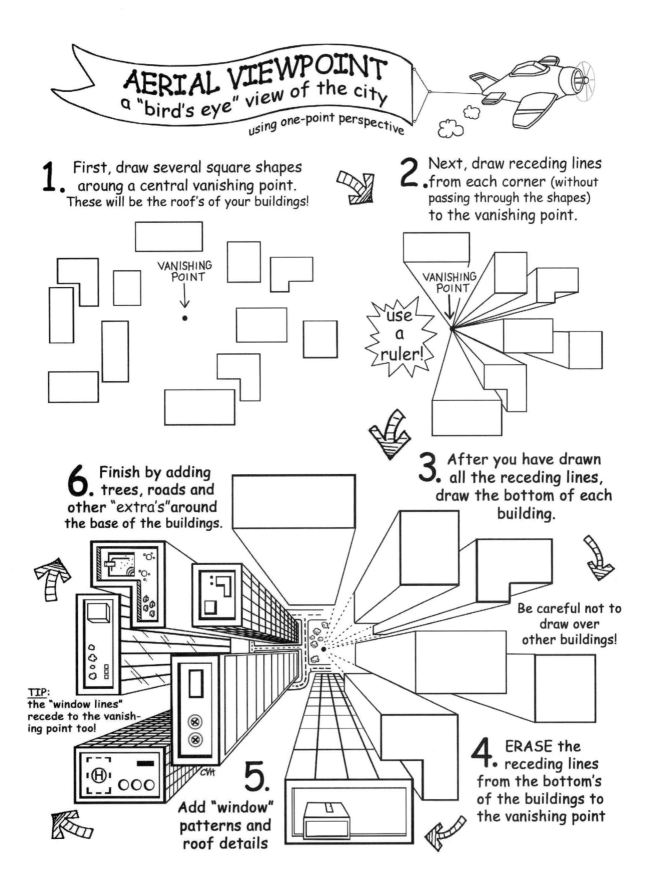

AERIAL VIEWPOINT
a "bird's eye" view of the city
using one-point perspective

1. First, draw several square shapes aroung a central vanishing point. These will be the roof's of your buildings!

VANISHING POINT

2. Next, draw receding lines from each corner (without passing through the shapes) to the vanishing point.

VANISHING POINT

use a ruler!

3. After you have drawn all the receding lines, draw the bottom of each building.

Be careful not to draw over other buildings!

4. ERASE the receding lines from the bottom's of the buildings to the vanishing point

5. Add "window" patterns and roof details

6. Finish by adding trees, roads and other "extra's" around the base of the buildings.

TIP: the "window lines" recede to the vanishing point too!

CVA

BLOCK LETTER PERSPECTIVE

KNOW:
Differences between near and far objects in a scene

UNDERSTAND:
• The illusion of depth can be created using one point perspective techniques

DO:
• Following the techniques provided, create the illusion of 3D lettering using one point perspective, receding lines and block letters to write your name
• Shade and add a bevel edge

TIP: Try to create sharp corners on your letters so the edges are not rounded. Rounded edges are more difficult to create perspective with. As you practice and get better, try using rounded bubble letters.

Use a ruler!

BLOCK LETTERS: Draw your name using perspective

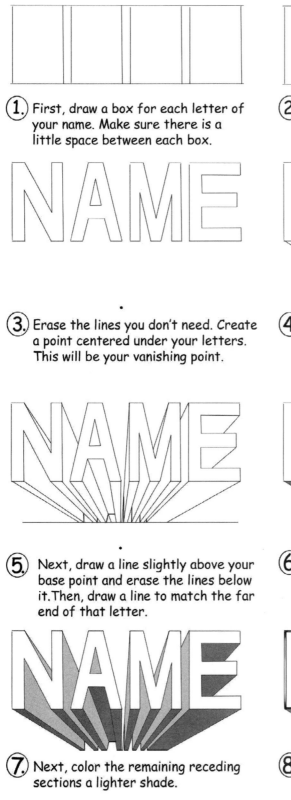

① First, draw a box for each letter of your name. Make sure there is a little space between each box.

② Next, "carve" out your letters from each box. Use the edges of the box as part of each letter as needed.

③ Erase the lines you don't need. Create a point centered under your letters. This will be your vanishing point.

④ With a ruler, line up each corner of each letter to the vanishing point and draw a line. Stop your line when it touches another letter. It helps to do all the bottoms of the letters first.

⑤ Next, draw a line slightly above your base point and erase the lines below it. Then, draw a line to match the far end of that letter.

⑥ Erase the lines you don't need. Shade the bottom of each receding letter section a dark shade.

⑦ Next, color the remaining receding sections a lighter shade.

⑧ Finish it off by adding a bevel line inside each letter. Shade for a "carved" look.

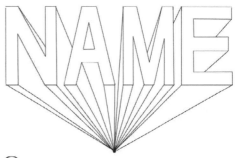

Block Letter

Alphabet "Cheat Sheet"

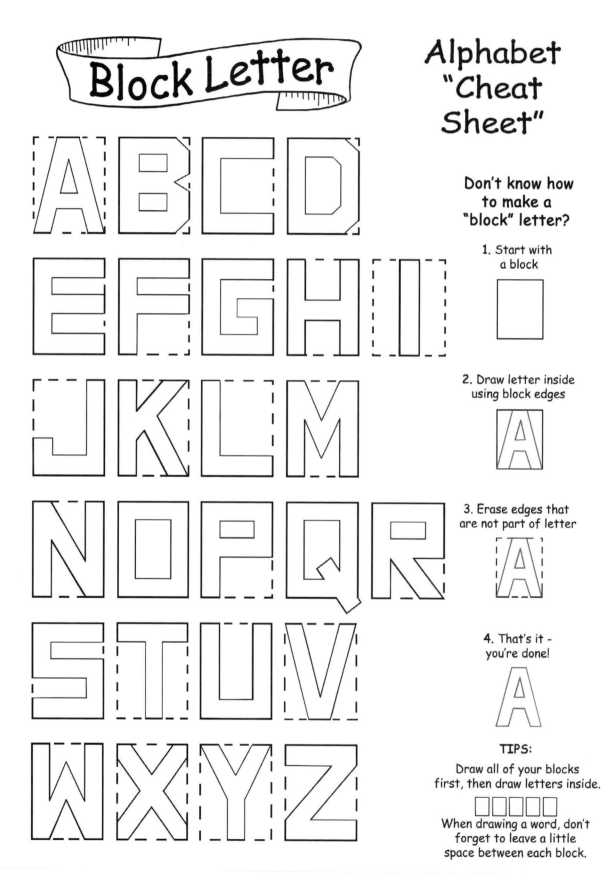

Don't know how to make a "block" letter?

1. Start with a block

2. Draw letter inside using block edges

3. Erase edges that are not part of letter

4. That's it - you're done!

TIPS:

Draw all of your blocks first, then draw letters inside.

When drawing a word, don't forget to leave a little space between each block.

DRAW AN ICEBERG

KNOW:
How to create a sense of depth in an artwork

UNDERSTAND:
• Overlapping and differences in the size of objects in a scene help to achieve the illusion of depth
• Drawn objects that appear close to us are large and usually close to the bottom of the page. Objects that appear farther from us in a drawing are usually small and higher on the page.

DO:
Create an original artwork showing overlapping and depth including at least 3 icebergs of differing sizes, water ripples and a horizon line

VOCABULARY:
Horizon Line - A line where water or land appears to end and the sky begins
Organic Shape - An irregular shape that might be found in nature
Perspective - The technique used to create the illusion of 3D onto a 2D surface. Perspective helps to create a sense of depth or receding space.

Draw an Iceberg

1. Start with an organic shape

random curves

2. Add vertical lines at every curve going downward

curved inward slightly

3. Connect the verticals you just made with a curved base

round slightly

4. Add some more smaller organic shapes higher up on the page

tiny one here

5. Connect the smaller shapes with vertical lines

background icebergs thinner than foreground icebergs

6. Shade

"motion" ripples

shade dark at top lighter at bottom

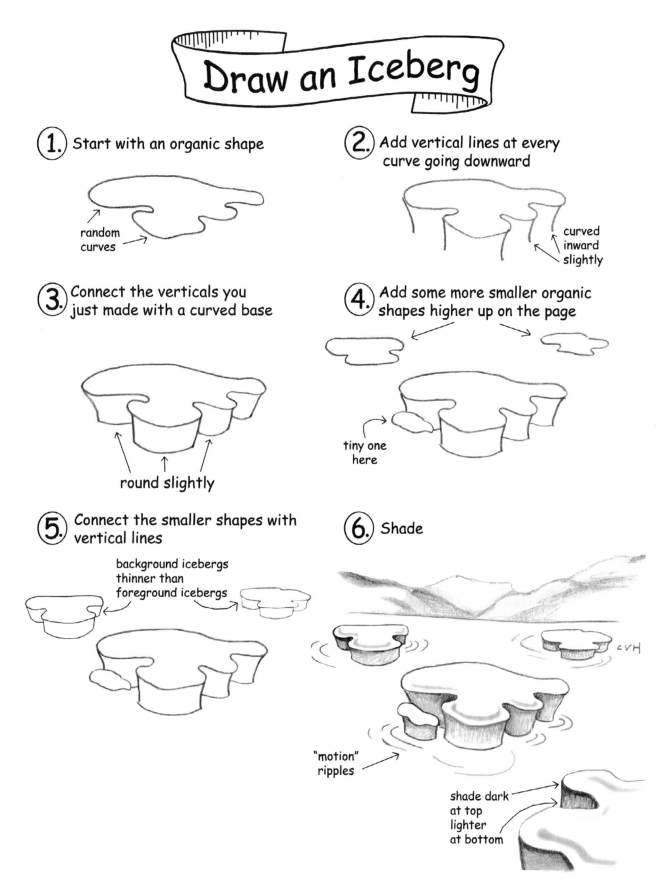

DRAW 2 TURNTABLES

KNOW:
Another way to use receding lines and create a sense of depth in an artwork

UNDERSTAND:
Drawn objects that appear close to us are large and usually close to the bottom of the page. Objects that appear farther from us in a drawing are small and higher on the page. Even if single items can portray depth when the "closer" parts are drawn large and the "far" parts are drawn small.

DO:
Create an original artwork of 2 turntables as seen in the handout

VOCABULARY:
Perspective - The technique used to create the illusion of 3D onto a 2D surface. Perspective helps to create a sense of depth or receding space.

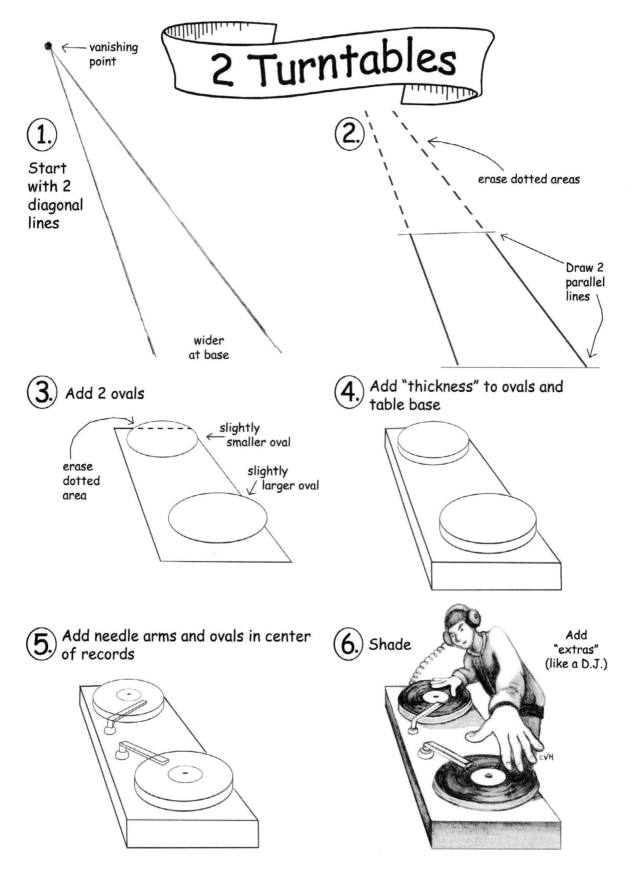

2 Turntables

vanishing point

1. Start with 2 diagonal lines

wider at base

2. erase dotted areas

Draw 2 parallel lines

3. Add 2 ovals

slightly smaller oval

erase dotted area

slightly larger oval

4. Add "thickness" to ovals and table base

5. Add needle arms and ovals in center of records

6. Shade

Add "extras" (like a D.J.)

CVH

AN OPEN BOOK

KNOW:
Receding lines help to create the illusion of depth

UNDERSTAND:
• The portion of a drawn object that is closest to the bottom of the page appears larger than the rest
• Adding a curve to straight lines of an object in a drawing creates interest and realism

DO:
Create an original artwork of an open book using learned techniques. Add "extra's" like a candle, quill pen and inkwell or text on the pages.

VOCABULARY:
Perspective - The technique used to create the illusion of 3D onto a 2D surface. Perspective helps to create a sense of depth or receding space.
Receding Line - A line that goes back into space

An Open Book

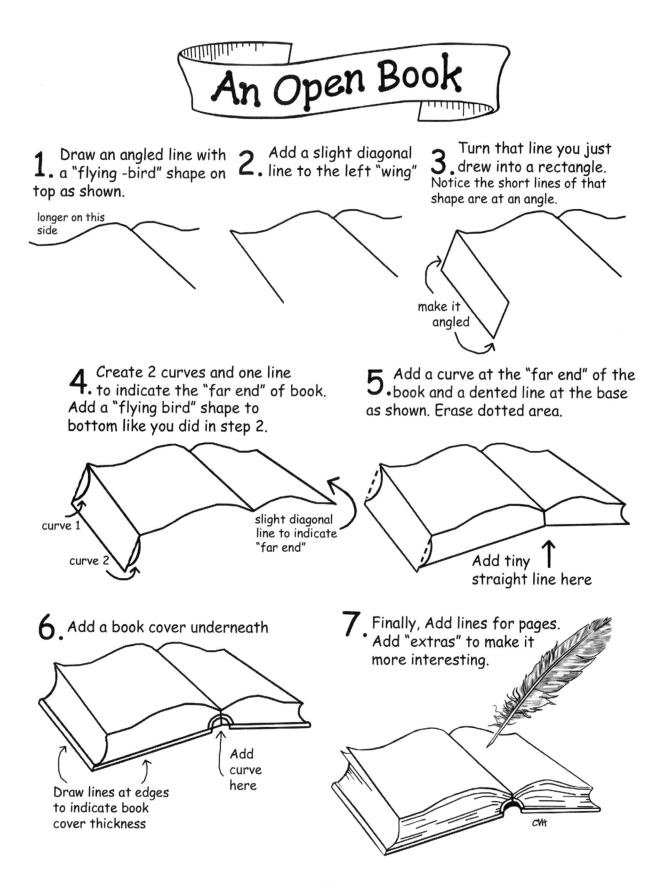

1. Draw an angled line with a "flying-bird" shape on top as shown.

longer on this side

2. Add a slight diagonal line to the left "wing"

3. Turn that line you just drew into a rectangle. Notice the short lines of that shape are at an angle.

make it angled

4. Create 2 curves and one line to indicate the "far end" of book. Add a "flying bird" shape to bottom like you did in step 2.

curve 1

curve 2

slight diagonal line to indicate "far end"

5. Add a curve at the "far end" of the book and a dented line at the base as shown. Erase dotted area.

Add tiny straight line here

6. Add a book cover underneath

Draw lines at edges to indicate book cover thickness

Add curve here

7. Finally, Add lines for pages. Add "extras" to make it more interesting.

CVH

OPEN GATES

KNOW:
Vertical lines, Parallel lines

UNDERSTAND:
In most architectural drawings, vertical lines are all parallel or the horizontals are all parallel. Rarely are both types of lines perfectly parallel and straight in the same drawing. In this case, all of the vertical lines are perfectly straight and parallel, the horizontals are not.

DO:
Create an original artwork of opening gates using learned techniques. Add "extra's" like a scroll design, bars, brickwork, etc.

VOCABULARY:
Architectural Drawings - Drawings that depict human-made buildings
Horizontal - Straight and flat across, parallel to the horizon. The opposite is vertical.
Parallel - Two or more straight lines or edges on the same plane that do not intersect. Parallel lines have the same direction.
Perspective - The technique used to create the illusion of 3D onto a 2D surface. Perspective helps to create a sense of depth or receding space.
Vertical Line - The direction going straight up and down

Open Gates
Fancy or Not

use a ruler!

1. Start with an angled rectangle like this one

angled downward here

angled upward here

2. Repeat that shape, but this time make it a mirror image

angled down-ward here

angled upward toward the center

3. Add a skinny rectangle on each side and 2 lines inside each gate (angled upward)

4. Add parallel lines that are close together inside the gate.

Erase insides here

5. Add fancy scrolls inside gate and on top if you want. Use your imagination!

Add a few rectangles for "bricks" inside pillar

Extend fence on both sides if you have space

CVH

97

Chapter 4

Holidays & Seasons

VALENTINE
Heart Lock and Key

KNOW:
Drawing objects viewed at various angles can add interest to a work

UNDERSTAND:

• How to add depth and interest to a drawn object
• How to take simple shapes and change them into more complex items

DO:
Create an original artwork of a heart shaped lock with an old fashioned key

VOCABULARY:
Depth - The third dimension. The apparent distance from front to back or near to far in an artwork.
Perspective - The technique used to create the illusion of 3D onto a 2D surface. Perspective helps to create a sense of depth or receding space.

Heart Lock with Key

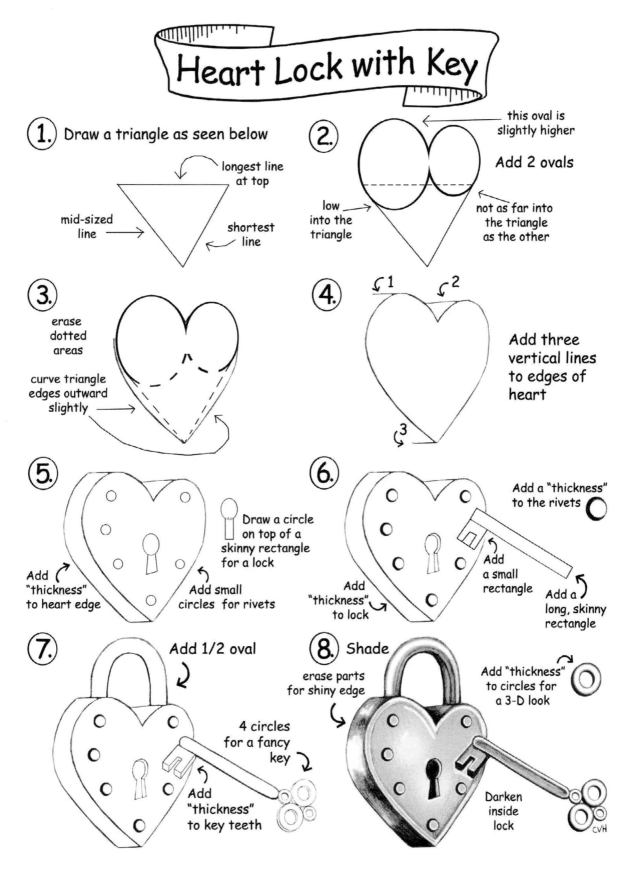

1. Draw a triangle as seen below

longest line at top

mid-sized line →

← shortest line

2. this oval is slightly higher

Add 2 ovals

low into the triangle →

← not as far into the triangle as the other

3. erase dotted areas

curve triangle edges outward slightly →

4. 1 2 3

Add three vertical lines to edges of heart

5. Draw a circle on top of a skinny rectangle for a lock

Add "thickness" to heart edge

Add small circles for rivets

6. Add a "thickness" to the rivets

Add a small rectangle

Add "thickness" to lock

Add a long, skinny rectangle

7. Add 1/2 oval

4 circles for a fancy key

Add "thickness" to key teeth

8. Shade

erase parts for shiny edge

Add "thickness" to circles for a 3-D look

Darken inside lock

CVH

101

ROSE

KNOW:
The difference between geometric and organic shapes

UNDERSTAND:
Connecting a series of simple geometric shapes can create a complex (organic) object

DO:
Create an original artwork of a rose using the techniques provided

VOCABULARY:
Asymmetry - An object is different on both sides

Balance - A principle of design, balance refers to the way the elements of art are arranged to create a feeling of stability in a work

Geometric Shape - Any shape or form having more mathematic than organic design. Geometric designs are typically made with straight lines.

Organic Shape - An irregular shape that might be found in nature, rather than a mechanical or angular shape

How to Draw a Rose

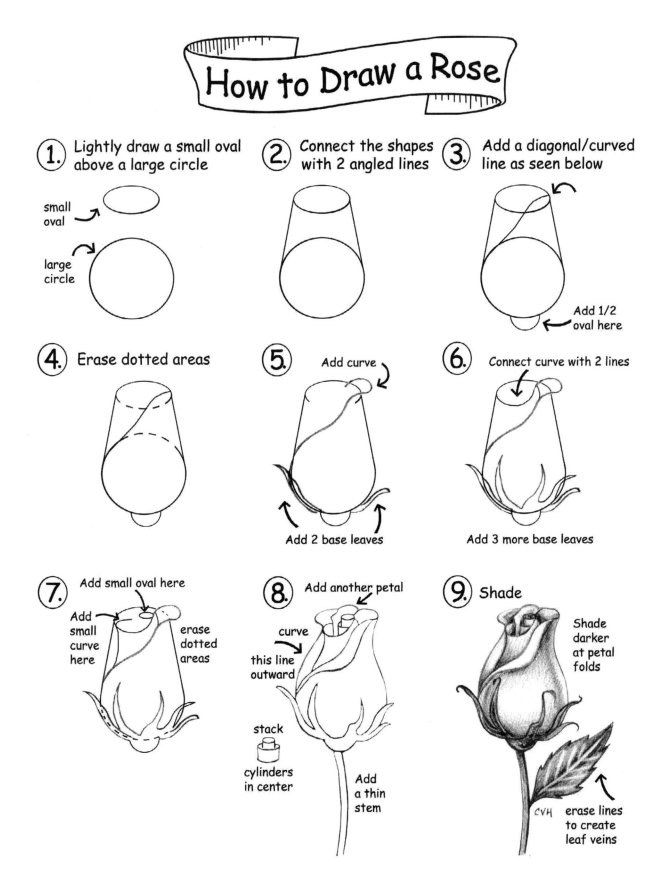

1. Lightly draw a small oval above a large circle

small oval

large circle

2. Connect the shapes with 2 angled lines

3. Add a diagonal/curved line as seen below

Add 1/2 oval here

4. Erase dotted areas

5. Add curve

Add 2 base leaves

6. Connect curve with 2 lines

Add 3 more base leaves

7. Add small oval here

Add small curve here

erase dotted areas

8. Add another petal

curve this line outward

stack cylinders in center

Add a thin stem

9. Shade

Shade darker at petal folds

CVH   erase lines to create leaf veins

LOVE SWANS

KNOW:

Mirror symmetry

UNDERSTAND:

• Mirror symmetry is when the parts of an image or object are organized so that one side duplicates (mirrors) the other
• Perfect symmetry is rarely found in nature

DO:

Students will try and create a symmetrical design of "Love Swans" using simple shapes and the tips and tricks provided

VOCABULARY:

Mirror Symmetry - The parts of an image or object organized so that one side duplicates, or mirrors, the other. Also known as formal balance, its opposite is asymmetry or asymmetrical balance.
Symmetry is among the ten classes of patterns

Whatever you do
to one side,
try and match it
on the other . . .

Love Swans

using
Mirror
Symmetry

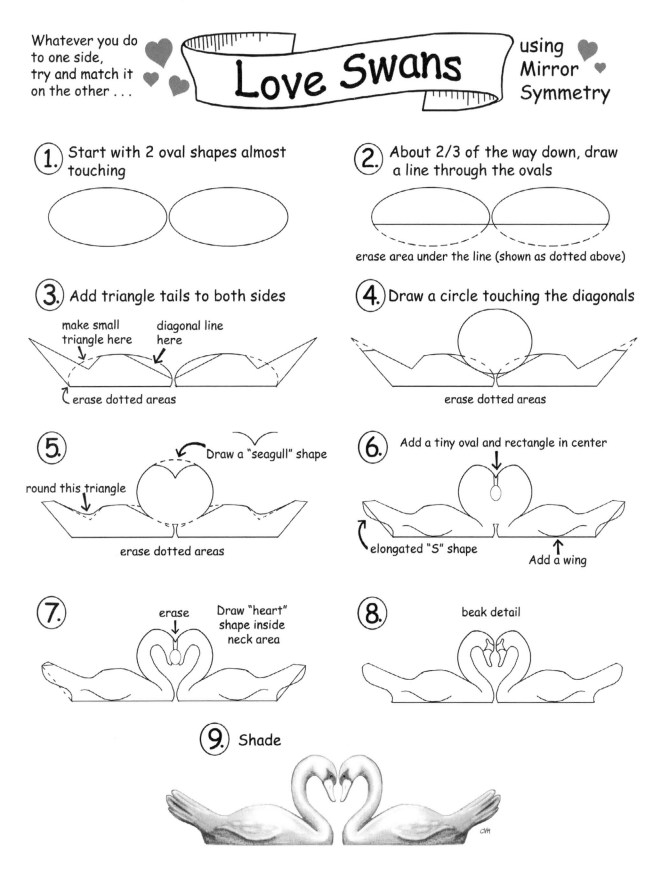

1. Start with 2 oval shapes almost touching

2. About 2/3 of the way down, draw a line through the ovals

erase area under the line (shown as dotted above)

3. Add triangle tails to both sides

make small triangle here

diagonal line here

erase dotted areas

4. Draw a circle touching the diagonals

erase dotted areas

5. Draw a "seagull" shape

round this triangle

erase dotted areas

6. Add a tiny oval and rectangle in center

elongated "S" shape

Add a wing

7. erase

Draw "heart" shape inside neck area

8. beak detail

9. Shade

CVH

105

BARBED WIRE HEART

KNOW:
Connecting a few simple geometric shapes can create a more complex object

UNDERSTAND:
Using overlapping techniques to give an object the appearance of form

DO:
Create an original heart drawing wrapped in barbed wire. Use curved, overlapping lines on top of the heart to give the illusion of "wrapping" and depth.

VOCABULARY:
Form - An element of art that is three-dimensional (height, width, and depth) and encloses volume

Overlap - When one thing lies over, partly covering something else. Depicting this is one of the most important means of conveying an illusion of depth. (Other means include varying sizes and placement on a receding plane, along with linear and aerial perspective.)

Barbed Wire Heart

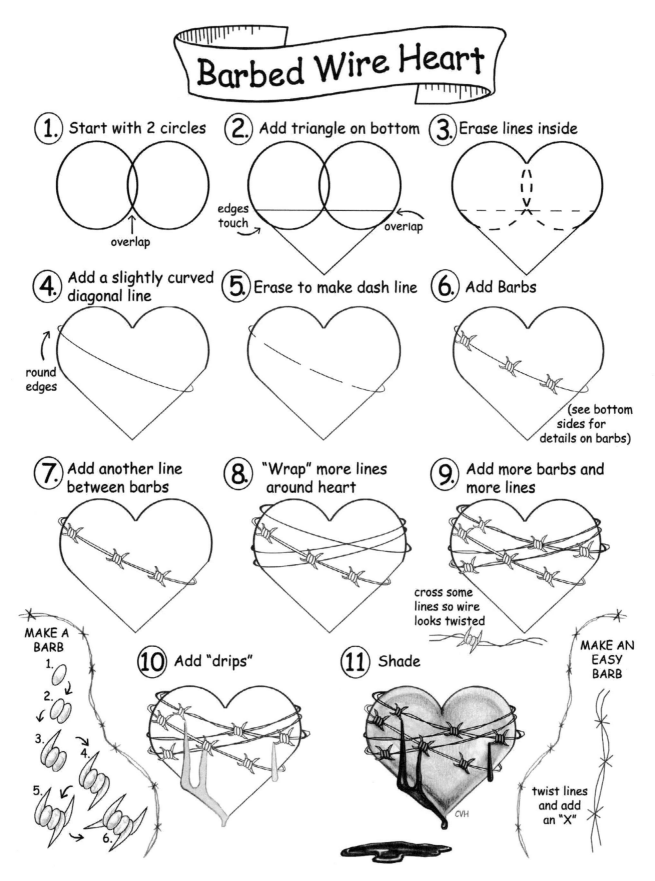

1. Start with 2 circles

overlap

2. Add triangle on bottom

edges touch

overlap

3. Erase lines inside

4. Add a slightly curved diagonal line

round edges

5. Erase to make dash line

6. Add Barbs

(see bottom sides for details on barbs)

7. Add another line between barbs

8. "Wrap" more lines around heart

9. Add more barbs and more lines

cross some lines so wire looks twisted

MAKE A BARB
1.
2.
3.
4.
5.
6.

10 Add "drips"

11 Shade

CVH

MAKE AN EASY BARB

twist lines and add an "X"

107

SCROLL AND ROSE

KNOW:
• Connecting a series of simple geometric shapes can create a complex (organic) object
• Curving lines indicate perspective via overlapping

UNDERSTAND:

• Overlapping and differences in the size of objects in a scene help to achieve the illusion of depth
• High contrast shading gives the appearance of form and 3D

DO:
Follow the steps on the handout provided to create your own version of a banner wrapping around a rose blossom. Add a message on the banner and shade.

VOCABULARY:
High Contrast Shading - A large difference between dark and light values in an art-work (fewer mid-tones)
Overlap - When one thing lies over or partly covers something else

Scroll and Rose

1. Start with a spiral

2. Add a base (looks like a wine glass)

3. Add "wings" and 3 petals

"wings"

4. "Thicken" wings

5. Add curvy bottom petals and stem nub

6. The rose is done! Next, start scroll

angled curvy line

7. Vertical lines from each curve

make 6 vertical lines

8. Make bottom and ends of scroll

Jagged edge on leaves

9. Add a stem, leaves and lettering Shade it!

Love to Draw

CVH

erase lines to create leaf veins

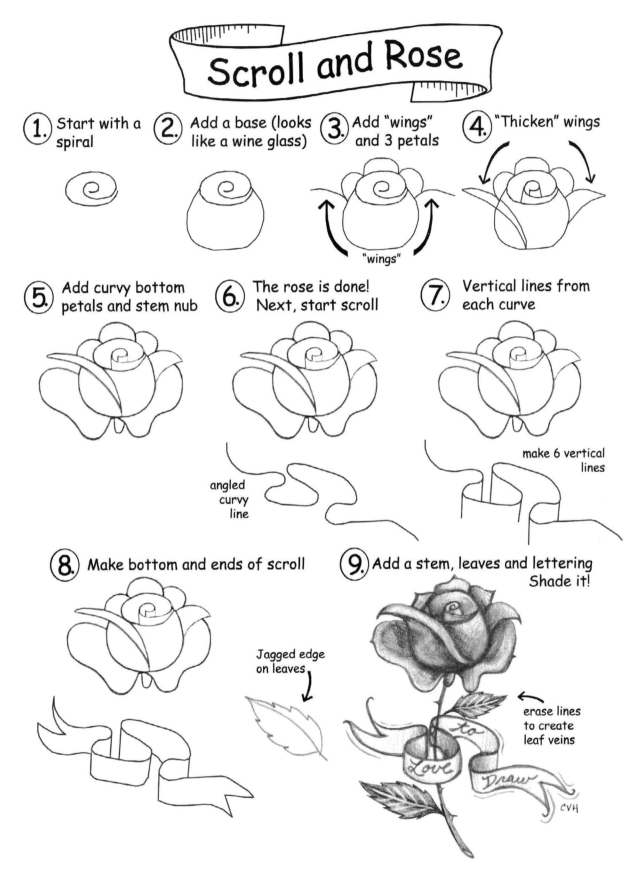

POT O' GOLD

KNOW:
• Simple shapes combined together can create more complex objects
• Many objects (man made and natural) are based on the cylinder

UNDERSTAND:

• Disks are short cylinders
• Using the principles of a cylinder (rounded base and an ellipse top) can create a variety of shapes when used in drawing

DO:
Create the illusion of a 3D pot filled with "disks" of gold coins. Shade.

VOCABULARY:
Cylinder - A tube that appears three-dimensional
Disk - A 3D oval
Ellipse - A circle viewed at an angle (drawn as an oval)

Pot O'Gold

1. Start with an oval

2. Add the bottom of a circle shape

3. Rim bottom of oval with a "thickness"

4. Add inner rim "thickness" at top

5. tiny circle — legs

6. Add curved handle — 3-D coin

2 ways to make a 3-D coin
Try them both and see which way you like best!

1. Oval
2. Add another
3. Erase dotted area
4. Add detail

— OR —

1. Oval
2. Add 2 lines
3. Connect

CVH

111

CUTE EASTER STUFF

KNOW:
• Simple shapes combined together can create complex objects
• A cross section of a cone can create a vessel
• Adding "hatch" lines to the inside of an outlined object give it form, volume and shadow

UNDERSTAND:
• Technique of "hatching" and "cross-hatching" to show shadow, texture or form in an object
• Texture is used by artists to show how something might feel or what it is made of

DO:
Create an artwork including the objects outlined on the handout. Add "extra's". Try hatching detail for texture and shading.

VOCABULARY:
Cone - Two lines at the edge of an ellipse that eventually meet
Hatching - A series of closely spaced parallel lines. When more lines are placed at an angle on top of those lines, it is called cross-hatching.
Texture - The way something looks like it might feel like in an artwork
Volume - The space within a form

Cute Easter Stuff

1. Start with an oval

2. Add another overlapping oval

erase dotted area

3. Add 2 smaller 1/2 circles at base

4. Add triangle beak

erase

5. Add eye and 2 thin legs

6. Add 3 toes to each leg

7. Make outer edges "fluffy" with hatch lines

8. Shade

CVH

Easter Basket

1. Start with 2 ovals

bigger

smaller

2. Connect sides

erase dotted area

3. Add 1/2 oval for handle

4. Shade

EASTER EGGS

KNOW:
Taking a shape and turning in into a form by adding contour lines, pattern and shading

UNDERSTAND:
The technique of "wrapping" lines and pattern around an object so that it appears 3D

DO:
Create an original pattern "wrapped" around a shape to create a festive holiday egg form. Try creating a basket of eggs as seen in the handout.

VOCABULARY:
Pattern - The repetition of shapes, lines, or colors in a design
Repetition - A way of combining elements of art so that the same elements are used over and over again
Wrap - The appearance of something curving around another object

Easter Eggs

1. Start with a basic egg shape

narrow at top

wider at base

2. Add curves lines to show depth

3. Add a decoration or pattern

or try these . . .

Add color or shade

BASKET OF EGGS

Start with a couple of eggs

Add more <u>under</u> them

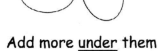
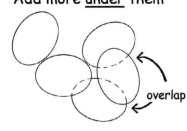

overlap

Add more . . .

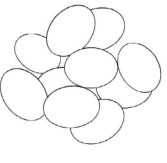

Decorate and shade

CVH

SPRING TULIP

KNOW:
• Connecting a series of simple geometric shapes can create a complex (organic) object
• The difference between geometric and organic shapes
• Line can indicate perspective via overlapping

UNDERSTAND:
• Overlapping and differences in the size of objects in a scene help to achieve the illusion of depth
• High contrast shading gives the appearance of form and 3D

DO:
Draw your version of a Spring Tulip bouquet using the tips and tricks provided. Draw at least 3 flowers. Add something you don't see on the worksheet to make your artwork unique (i.e. a vase, stems tied with a ribbon, etc.) Don't trace. Shade.

VOCABULARY:
High Contrast Shading - A large difference between dark and light values in an artwork (fewer mid-tones)
Overlap - When one thing lies over or partly covers something else

Spring Tulip

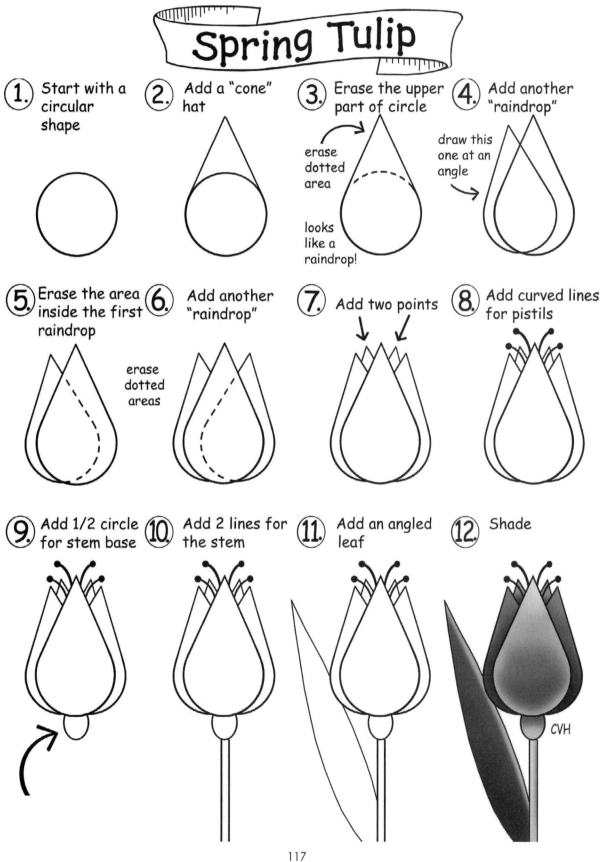

1. Start with a circular shape

2. Add a "cone" hat

3. Erase the upper part of circle
   erase dotted area
   looks like a raindrop!

4. Add another "raindrop"
   draw this one at an angle

5. Erase the area inside the first raindrop

6. Add another "raindrop"
   erase dotted areas

7. Add two points

8. Add curved lines for pistils

9. Add 1/2 circle for stem base

10. Add 2 lines for the stem

11. Add an angled leaf

12. Shade

CVH

117

CHERRY BLOSSOM

KNOW:
Balance, Organic Shape, Pattern, Perspective, Repetition, Symmetry/Asymmetry

UNDERSTAND:
• Overlapping simple shapes can be the first step to creating complex forms
• Simplifying an artwork consists of breaking down the major parts of an object into simple shapes. Once the simple shapes are discovered, more detail can be added.

DO:
• Follow the steps provided to create an original still life drawing of cherry blossoms
• Start with contour lines and simple geometric shapes and overlap as needed to create realism
• Shade with pencil (or watercolor pencils and use as directed)

VOCABULARY:
Organic - An irregular shape that might be found in nature, rather than a regular, mechanical shape
Perspective - The technique used to create the illusion of 3D onto a 2D surface. Perspective helps to create a sense of depth or receding space.
Still Life - A drawing, painting or photo of inanimate objects positioned on a table (traditionally vessels, fruits, vegetables, etc.)
Symmetry - An object that is the same on both sides

Cherry Blossoms

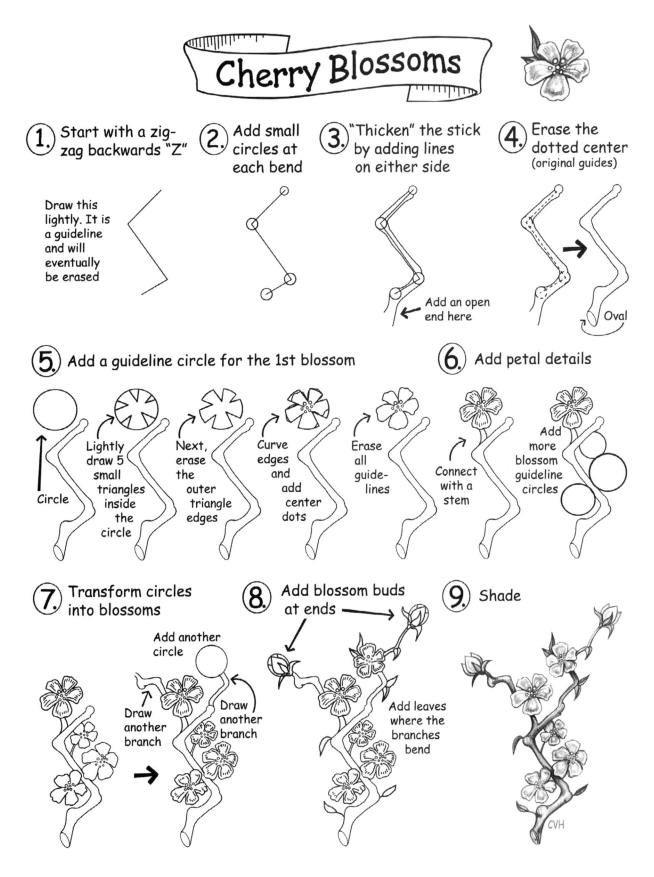

1. Start with a zig-zag backwards "Z"

Draw this lightly. It is a guideline and will eventually be erased

2. Add small circles at each bend

3. "Thicken" the stick by adding lines on either side

Add an open end here

4. Erase the dotted center (original guides)

Oval

5. Add a guideline circle for the 1st blossom

Circle

Lightly draw 5 small triangles inside the circle

Next, erase the outer triangle edges

Curve edges and add center dots

Erase all guidelines

Connect with a stem

Add more blossom guideline circles

6. Add petal details

7. Transform circles into blossoms

Add another circle

Draw another branch

Draw another branch

8. Add blossom buds at ends

Add leaves where the branches bend

9. Shade

CVH

119

HALLOWEEN CREATURES

KNOW:
You can make simple and original cartoon-style creatures by using simple, geometric shapes

UNDERSTAND:
• To make a work original, that work must have elements that are not copied or traced
• Expressive qualities in your drawing add a feeling, mood or idea to your character

DO:
Practice creating an original, Halloween themed cartoon-style character using the geometric guidelines provided. Draw lightly so guidelines can be erased if needed. Add or change certain elements as necessary to make it unique. Try to create a character NOT seen on the handout. Use your imagination and add a lot of "extra's".

VOCABULARY:
Cartoon - A usually simple drawing created to get people thinking, angry, laughing, or otherwise amused. A cartoon usually has simple lines, uses basic colors, and tells a story in one or a series of pictures called frames or panels.

Expressive Qualities - The feelings, moods and ideas communicated to the viewer through a work of art

Original - Any work considered to be an authentic example of the works of an artist, rather than a reproduction, imitation or a copy

TRICK OR TREAT

Halloween Creatures

A little **SCARY** but mostly cute!

1. Start with a body made from simple shapes . . .

2. Next, choose an expressive set of eyes . . .

3. Finally, add as many details as you need to build a unique, interesting character

erase guidelines as needed

More Creatures . . .

AUTUMN LEAF

KNOW:
Organic Shape, Symmetry, Asymmetry

UNDERSTAND:
Overlapping simple shapes can be the first step to creating complex forms

DO:
• Follow the steps provided (or position a selection leaves from life) to create an original still life drawing
• Start with contour lines and simple geometric shapes and overlap as needed to create guidelines
• Shade with pencil (or watercolor pencils and use as directed)

VOCABULARY:
Organic - An irregular shape that might be found in nature, rather than a regular, mechanical shape

Still Life - A drawing, painting or photo of inanimate objects positioned on a table (traditionally vessels, fruits, vegetables, etc.)

Symmetry - (or symmetrical balance) - The parts of an image or object organized so that one side duplicates, or mirrors, the other. Also known as formal balance, its opposite is asymmetry or asymmetrical balance.

Symmetry is among the ten classes of patterns.

Have a real leaf available?
Trace the contour of
that leaf and
skip to **step 6**

Autumn Leaf

1. Start with a tear-drop shape

2. Add 2 more tear-drop shapes fanned out at sides

3. Draw points around the tear-drop shapes as seen below

4. Erase the original tear-drop shape shown as dotted

5. It should look something like the organic shape below

6. Draw "veins" from the large points down to the center base

7. Add some smaller veins

8. Add more veins & stem

9. Shade

leaf tips can be darker

erase lines to create leaf veins

CVH

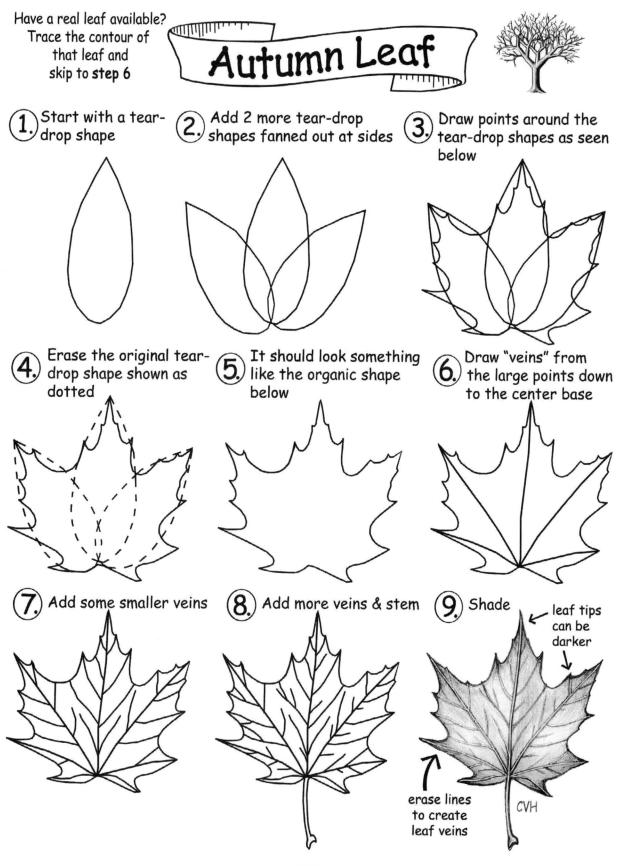

THANKSGIVING STILL LIFE

KNOW:
Contour Line, Overlapping, Perspective, "Still Life"

UNDERSTAND:
• Overlapping simple shapes is the first step to creating complex forms
• Large objects should be drawn lower on the page to appear close. Small objects should be drawn higher on the page to appear further away (fruits in the bowl).

DO:
• View and discuss examples of overlapping and images which have near and far elements, focusing on how overlap and size difference help to achieve an illusion of depth
• Follow the steps provided (or position a selection of fruits and vegetables from life) to create an original still life drawing with a "Thanksgiving" theme
• Start with contour lines and simple geometric shapes and overlap as needed to create guidelines
• Shade with pencil or watercolor pencils (use as directed)

VOCABULARY:
Contour Line - Lines that surround and define the edges of a subject
Overlap - When one thing lies over another, partly covering something else to convey depth or illusion
Shading - Showing change from light to dark or dark to light in a picture
Shape - An enclosed space
Still Life - A drawing, painting or photo of inanimate objects positioned on a table (traditionally vessels, fruits, vegetables, etc.)

Thanksgiving

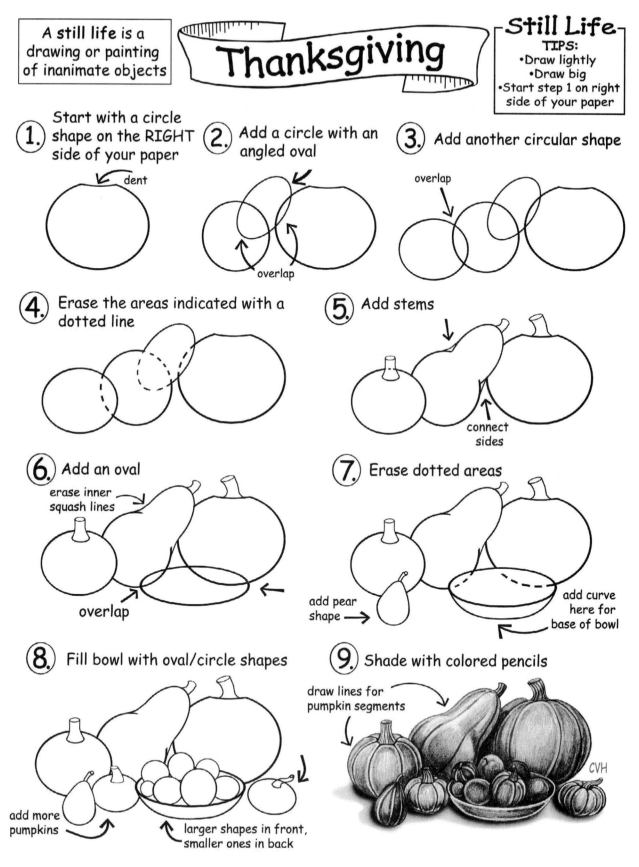

1. Start with a circle shape on the RIGHT side of your paper

dent

2. Add a circle with an angled oval

overlap

3. Add another circular shape

overlap

4. Erase the areas indicated with a dotted line

5. Add stems

connect sides

6. Add an oval

erase inner squash lines

overlap

7. Erase dotted areas

add pear shape →

add curve here for base of bowl

8. Fill bowl with oval/circle shapes

add more pumpkins

larger shapes in front, smaller ones in back

9. Shade with colored pencils

draw lines for pumpkin segments

CVH

125

CAN OF CRAN...

KNOW:
Cylinders, Pop Art

UNDERSTAND:
• Cylinders in art give the appearance of a 3D circular tube
• Warhol made the painting Campbell's Tomato Soup an icon of Pop Art in 1962

DO:
Create a cylindrical can using Warhol's "Pop Art" style. "Wrap" a label and text around the can to indicate 3D. Shade.

VOCABULARY:
Andy Warhol - (August 6, 1928 - February 22, 1987) was an American artist who was a leading figure in the visual art movement known as pop art. His works explore the relationship between artistic expression, celebrity culture and advertisement that flourished by the 1960s.

Cylinder - A tube that appears three-dimensional

Oval - A two-dimensional shape that looks like a circle that has been stretched to make it longer

Pop Art - An art movement that focuses attention upon familiar images of the popular culture such as billboards, comic strips, magazine advertisements, and supermarket products

Can of Cran . . .

1. Start with an oval

2. Add another oval

3. Connect with 2 horizontal lines

4. Draw a thin oval inside the top lid area to indicate a "thickness"

follow the contour of the bottom rim

5. Fill the lid with a series of lean ovals

6. Draw a rounded line to indicate the label area

7. Draw a light, curved line to indicate where your words will be

8. Sketch out your text

9. Shade

Dexter's
CAN-O-CRAN
THANKSGIVING
cranberry sauce

Dexter's
CAN-O-CRAN
THANKSGIVING
cranberry sauce

CVH

PUMPKIN

KNOW:
Shading, Layering, Foreshortening, Overlapping

UNDERSTAND:
• Value added to a shape (2D) when drawing creates form (3D)
• The lightness or darkness of a value indicates a light source on an object

DO:
Draw your version of a pumpkin using the tips and tricks provided. The center of your pumpkin should be lower on the page and the sides should appear to recede back to show foreshortening. Don't trace. Shade.

VOCABULARY:
Blend - To merge tones applied to a surface so that there is no crisp line indicating beginning or end of one tone

Foreshortening - A way of representing an object so that it conveys the illusion of depth, seeming to thrust forward or go back into space. Foreshortening's success often depends upon a point of view or perspective in which the sizes of near and far parts of a subject contrast greatly.

Overlapping - When one thing lies over another, partly covering something else

Shading - Showing change from light to dark or dark to light in a picture

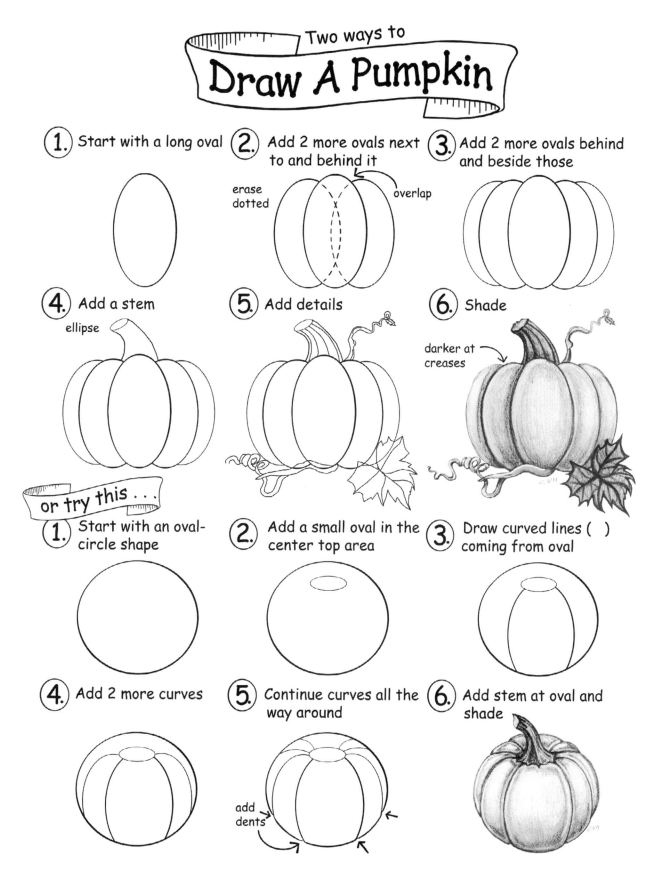

Two ways to
Draw A Pumpkin

1. Start with a long oval

2. Add 2 more ovals next to and behind it

erase dotted

overlap

3. Add 2 more ovals behind and beside those

4. Add a stem

ellipse

5. Add details

6. Shade

darker at creases

or try this . . .

1. Start with an oval-circle shape

2. Add a small oval in the center top area

3. Draw curved lines ( ) coming from oval

4. Add 2 more curves

5. Continue curves all the way around

add dents

6. Add stem at oval and shade

JACK O'LANTERN

KNOW:
Balance, Form, 3D

UNDERSTAND:
• Adding pattern and shading to an object give it form and dimension
• The use of receding lines to show perspective

DO:
Start with a basic pumpkin and then "carve" a design onto it using the tips and tricks provided. Add lots of "extra's" and be sure that all of the "carved" parts are connected - no floating pieces! Be original! Don't trace. Shade.

VOCABULARY:
Balance - The way the elements of art are arranged in an artwork to create a feeling of stability, a pleasing arrangement, or proportion of parts in a composition
Form - A three-dimensional shape (height, width, and depth) that encloses volume
Three-Dimensional - Having, or appearing to have, height, width, and depth

Jack O' Lantern

1. Start with a basic pumpkin outline

2. Draw the outline of eyes, nose and mouth

3. Erase any lines inside the eyes, nose and mouth

4. Draw short diagonal lines at corners of eyes, nose and mouth

5. Connect with angles to create a "thickness"

6. Shade

The lightest values should be in the "carved" holes to show that the pumpkin has a candle in it!

Get Creative

All of the "carved parts" must be connected ...no floating pieces!

CVH

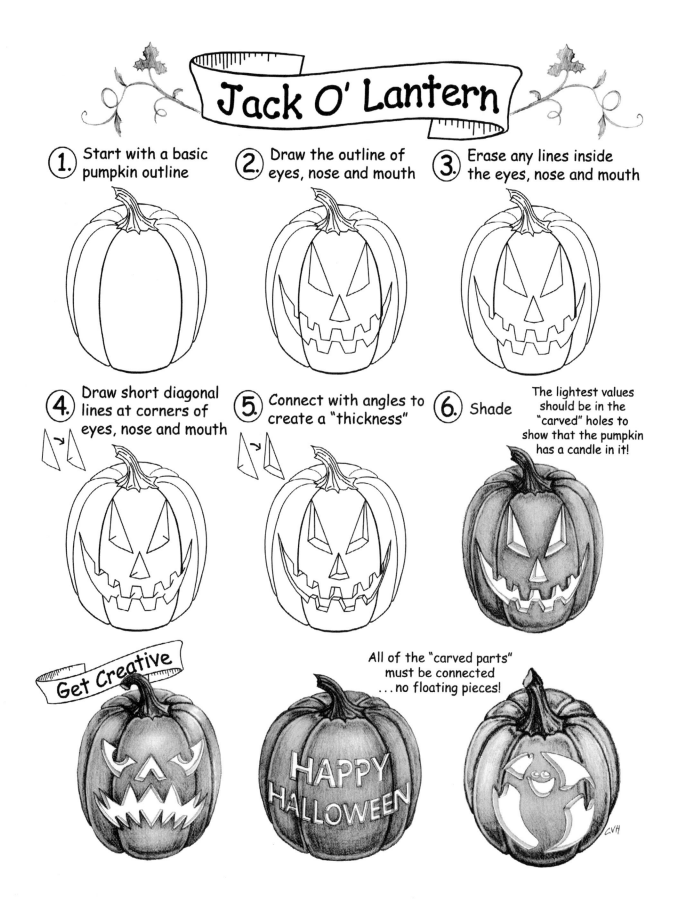

CHRISTMAS BARN

KNOW:
Simple steps to create a ¾ view of a house

UNDERSTAND:
One way to create the appearance of a 3D house showing perspective at a ¾ view

DO:
Create an original holiday barn in a landscape scene showing perspective. Add trees and shade.

VOCABULARY:
Landscape - An artwork which depicts scenery. There is usually some sky in the scene.
Perspective - The illusion of 3D on a 2D surface, creating a sense of depth and receding space
Three-Quarter (3/4) View - A view of a face or any other subject which is half-way between a full and a side view

Christmas Barn

1. Draw a rectangle (with shapes inside as seen below)

upward angle →

thinner here

wider here

2. Add 3 angled roof lines

← erase dotted area

3.

Add thickness ←

window

door

angle upward

← erase dotted

4. 3 lines for chimney

Add lines for doors and windows

5. top of chimney ←

circle for wreath

finish windows and door

6. Add windows and a tiny roof ←

7. Add trees

8. Shade

leave random white patches for snow

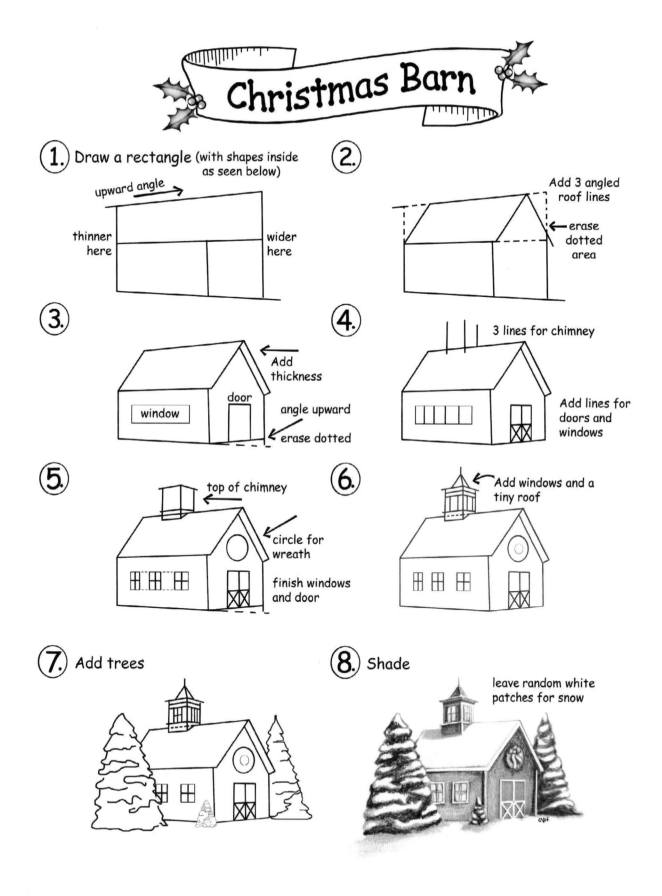

133

CHRISTMAS ORNAMENTS

KNOW:
Geometric shapes, Highlight, Repetition, Texture

UNDERSTAND:
• The difference between shape and form
• How to arrange elements in an artwork so that they appear symmetrical or equally balanced
• How to create an effective design using simple shapes
• How to create the appearance of texture

DO:
• Follow the steps provided to create an original ball ornament that starts with a simple circle connected to create a complex form
• Use learned 3D techniques which concentrate on overlapping and shading to convey the illusion of depth

VOCABULARY:
Balance - A principle of design, balance refers to the way the elements of art are arranged to create a feeling of stability in a work; a pleasing or harmonious arrangement or proportion of parts or areas in a design or composition.

Repetition - To continue a pattern over and over again

Texture - The technique an artist uses to make an object look like it feels a certain way

Christmas Ornaments

1. Start with a circle

2. Add a small oval directly above it

3. Add vertical lines decending from the oval edges

close with a curved line

4. Add a loop in the center of the oval

erase "behind" the cap (dotted area)

5. Add vertical lines on cap to show texture

6. Add a hook

and a shiny spot

Holly Berry border

TIP:
Holly leaves are green and berries are red

Create a greeting card using at least 3 ornaments

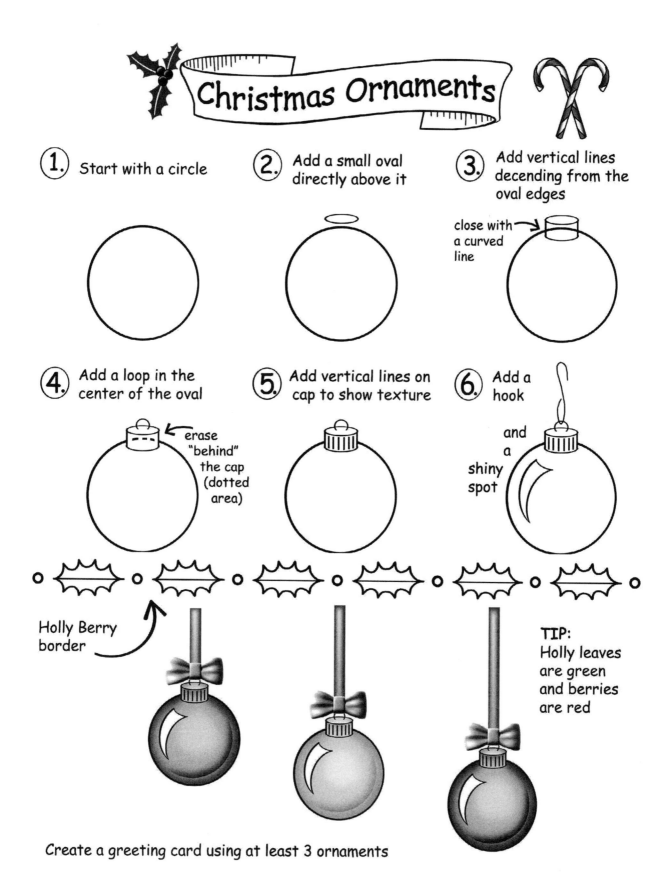

SIMPLE SNOWFLAKE

KNOW:
45 and 90 degree angles, Repetition, Rotational Symmetry

UNDERSTAND:
• No two snowflakes are alike
• Variation in sizes of objects when drawing them creates interest and depth
Optional: In fine art, a focal point highlights a specific portion of interest in an artwork

DO:
• Follow the steps provided to create an original snowflake design focusing on rotational symmetry
• Student will combine a variety of snowflakes styles and sizes to create a winter scene
Optional: Add a focal point using minimal color (colored pencil) in one or two areas of the scene to create interest

VOCABULARY:
Focal Point - The portion of an artwork's composition on which interest or attention centers. The focal point may be most interesting for any of several reasons: it may be given formal emphasis; its meaning may be controversial, incongruous, or otherwise compelling.

Rotational Symmetry - An object that looks the same after a certain amount of circular movement around that object's center

Symmetry - An object that is the same on both sides

Simple Snowflake

1. Use a ruler and draw a symmetrical cross

2. Draw a smaller "X" shape through the cross

this will create 8 equal 45° angles

3. Draw a line through each ending of the cross and "X" lines

4. Draw a tiny circle at the end of each "X" line

5. Add a 2nd, longer line through the ends of the cross and "X" lines

6. Add a small circle in the center

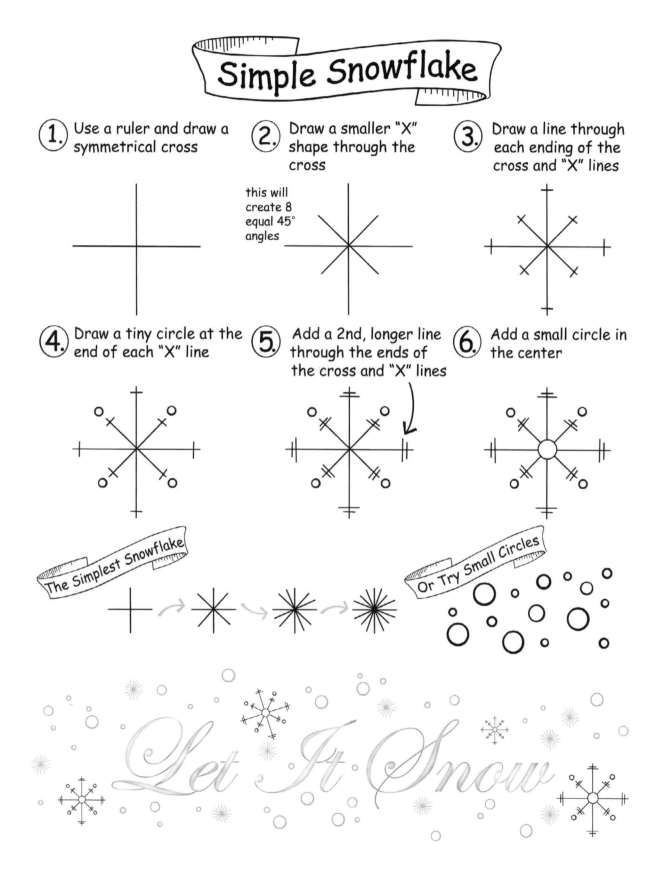

The Simplest Snowflake

Or Try Small Circles

Let It Snow

Chapter 5

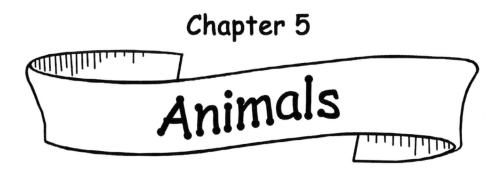

Animals

CARTOON ANIMALS

KNOW:
You can make almost ANY original cartoon creature using the steps provided

UNDERSTAND:
The basic, generic steps that can be changed or added to in order to make an ORIGINAL cartoon character

DO:
Create a front AND side view of a character NOT seen on the handout. Use your imagination and add a lot of "extra's".

VOCABULARY:
Cartoon - A usually simple drawing created to get people thinking, angry, laughing, or otherwise amused. A cartoon usually has simple lines, uses basic colors, and tells a story in one or a series of pictures called frames or panels.

Original - Any work considered to be an authentic example of the works of an artist, rather than a reproduction or imitation

Cartoon Animals

Follow these steps to make a front view of almost ANY cartoon creature!

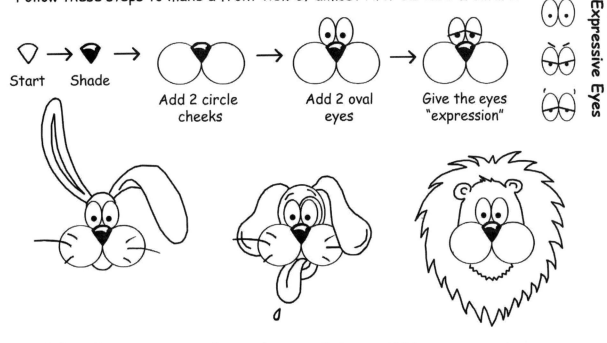

Start Shade

Add 2 circle cheeks

Add 2 oval eyes

Give the eyes "expression"

Expressive Eyes

Follow these steps to make a side view of almost ANY cartoon creature

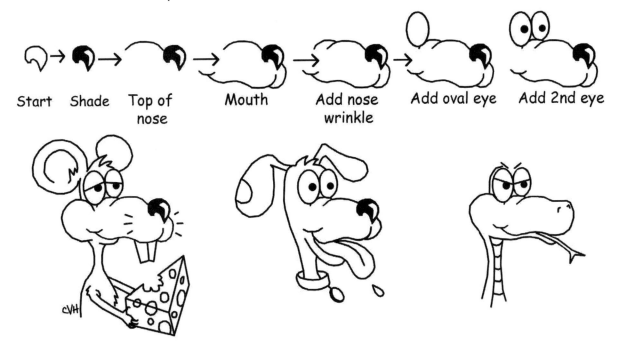

Start Shade Top of nose

Mouth

Add nose wrinkle

Add oval eye

Add 2nd eye

DUCK FAMILY

KNOW:
• How to create a sense of depth in an artwork
• How to take a few simple shapes and combine them to create a recognizable duck

UNDERSTAND:
• Overlapping and differences in the size and placement of objects in a scene can help to achieve the illusion of depth
• Lines, shapes, textures and shadows can be drawn to indicate a sense of motion in an artwork

DO:
Create an original artwork of a duck family including at least 1 large duck, 4 small ducks and water ripples to show movement in a landscape scene

VOCABULARY:
Landscape - An artwork which depicts scenery. There is usually some sky in the scene.
Perspective - The technique used to create the illusion of 3D onto a 2D surface. Perspective helps to create a sense of depth or receding space.

Duck Family

1. Start with a small circle

2. Add a rounded beak

3. Slightly curve neck

4. Add oval body

5. Triangle shaped tail

6. More tail detail . . .

7. Add front neck and chest

8. Erase dotted areas

9. Add an eye and water rings to indicate motion

ASSIGNMENT:
Draw 1 large duck and 4 smaller ducks in a pond

143

BUNNY RABBIT

KNOW:
Texture

UNDERSTAND:
The techniques an artist uses to show how something might feel or what it is made of in an artwork

DO:
Create an original artwork of a bunny rabbit indicating a "furry" texture with short hatch lines. Shade.

VOCABULARY:
Hatching - Closely spaced parallel lines
Texture - The way something looks like it might feel like in an artwork. Simulated textures are suggested by an artist with different brushstrokes, pencil lines, etc.

Some words describing various textures include: flat, smooth, shiny, glossy, glittery, velvety, feathery, soft, wet, gooey, furry, sandy, leathery, crackled, prickly, abrasive, rough, furry, bumpy, corrugated, puffy, rusty, slimy, etc.

Bunny Rabbit

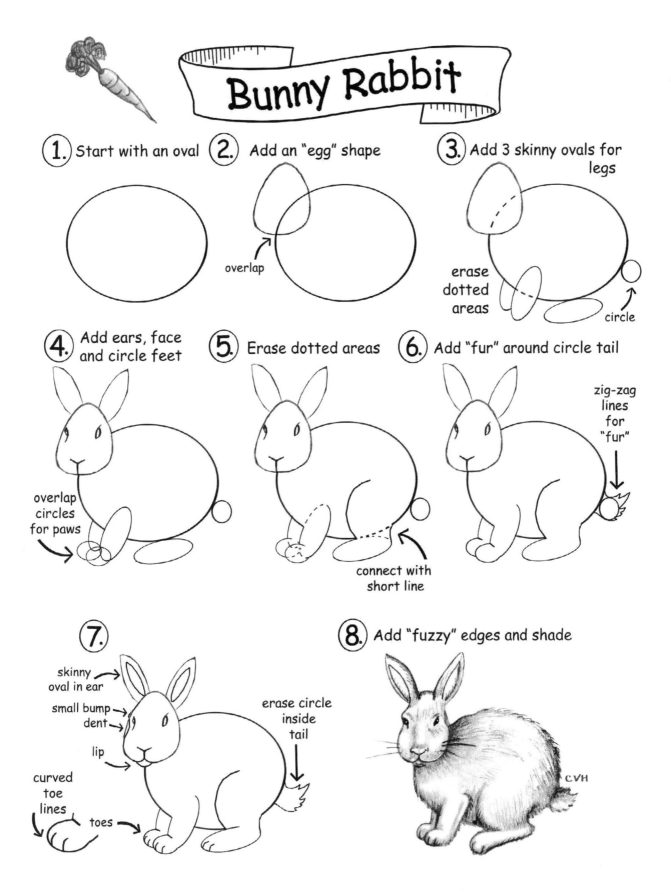

1. Start with an oval

2. Add an "egg" shape
overlap

3. Add 3 skinny ovals for legs
erase dotted areas
circle

4. Add ears, face and circle feet
overlap circles for paws

5. Erase dotted areas
connect with short line

6. Add "fur" around circle tail
zig-zag lines for "fur"

7.
skinny oval in ear
small bump
dent
lip
curved toe lines
toes
erase circle inside tail

8. Add "fuzzy" edges and shade
CVH

145

DRAW A PENGUIN

KNOW:
• Simple shapes combined together can create more complex objects
• Adding other elements to a drawing can create interest, tell a story, and detail (see "Perspective" chapter for iceberg instructions)

UNDERSTAND:
Overlapping and layering items help to create a sense of depth and realism

DO:
Create an original artwork of a penguin following the steps provided. Place him "on top" of an iceberg and put him in a scene.

VOCABULARY:
Detail - A part of a whole. A distinctive feature of an object or scene which can be seen most clearly close up.
Layer - Something placed over another surface
Overlap - When one thing lies over and partly covers something else

Draw a Penguin

1. Start with an oval

2. Add a small circle
← slightly off to one side

3. Connect with curved neck lines

4. Add skinny oval flippers
erase dotted area

5.
erase dotted area
"thicken" base →
Add "shark-fin" shape

6. Add beak and eye
erase dotted area
Add "triangle" feet

7.
Neck detail →
curves make webbed feet ↗
Add webbed toes →

8. Shade

cVH

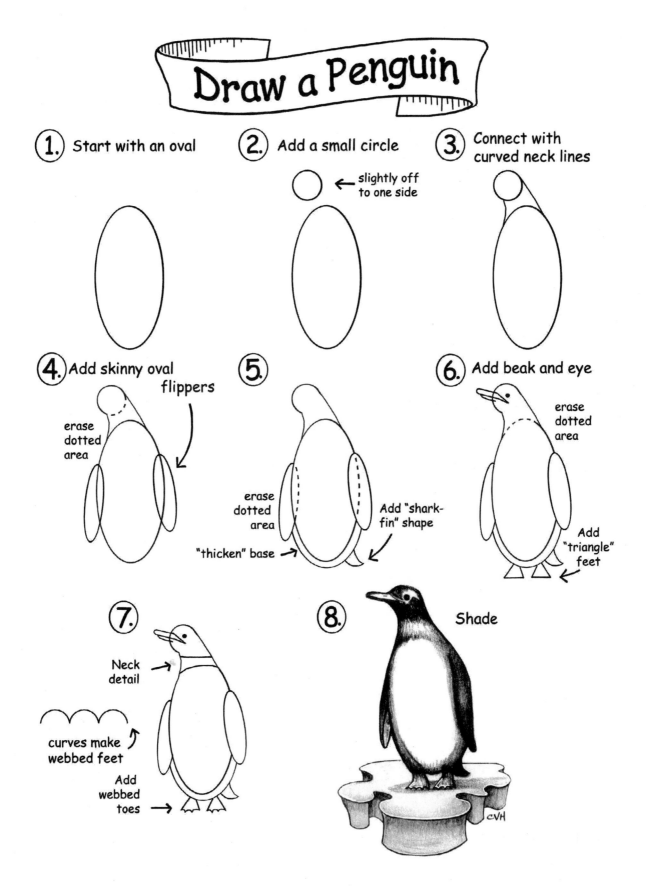

DRAWING WINGS

KNOW:
Symmetry and Asymmetry

UNDERSTAND:
Balance helps to create interest or design in an artwork. Symmetry and asymmetry offer two kinds of balance.

DO:
• Practice symmetry by drawing a creature with wings that are the same shape on both sides using the ideas provided
  OR
• Practice asymmetry by drawing a creature with wings that are at different positions on both sides using the ideas provided
• Add "extra's" like a halo, horns or pitchfork

VOCABULARY:
Asymmetry - An object is different on both sides
Balance - A principle of design, balance refers to the way the elements of art are arranged to create a feeling of stability in a work
Symmetry - One side of an object is the same as the other

Drawing Wings

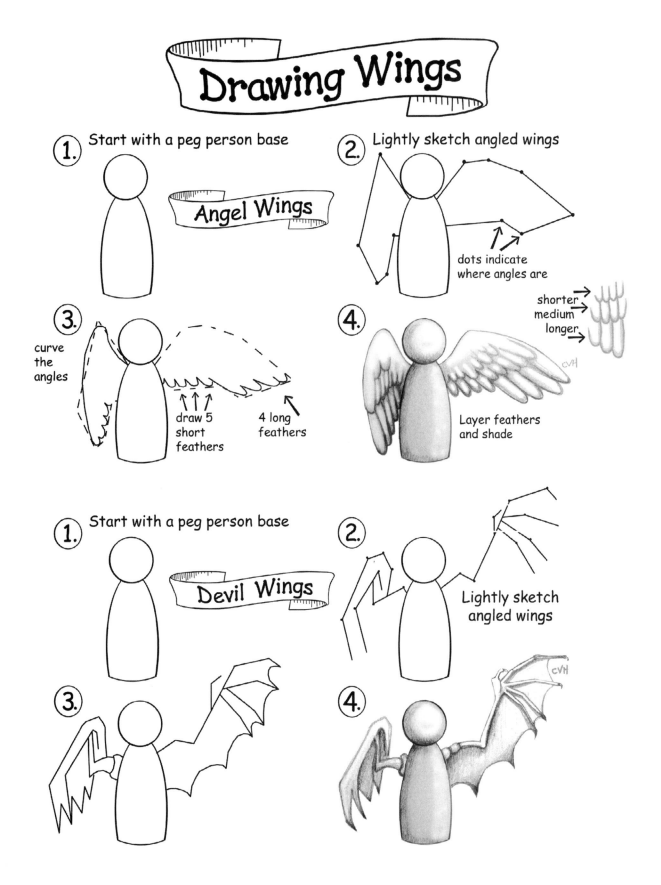

1. Start with a peg person base

Angel Wings

2. Lightly sketch angled wings

dots indicate where angles are

shorter
medium
longer

3. curve the angles

draw 5 short feathers

4 long feathers

4. Layer feathers and shade

1. Start with a peg person base

Devil Wings

2. Lightly sketch angled wings

3.

4.

149

BIRDS IN FLIGHT

KNOW:
Silhouette and Contour

UNDERSTAND:
• Silhouettes are detailed outlines but have no detail on the inside - just a solid block of color
• How to make a recognizable silhouette

DO:
Create an original landscape scene focusing on at least 3 silhouettes of birds in flight. Make sure there is a detailed outline of each bird including feather detail, head, body or tail.

TIP: Your silhouette has been drawn well if other people can see what it is!

VOCABULARY:
Contour - The outline and other visible edges of a drawn object
Silhouette - A detailed outline filled with a solid color, typically black on a white ground, and most often for a portrait

A silhouette is
a detailed outline

Birds in Flight

Below are three
samples of the many
types of bird
silhouettes you
can draw

1. Start with a wide "V" shape

2. Add a small circle in center bottom "V"

3. Thicken "V" and add tiny triangle tail

4. Fill in with a solid color and add "feather" detail to wing edges

1. Start with a wide "W" shape

2. "Thicken" the "W"

3. Add circle head and triangle tail

4. Fill in solid and add feather detail

1. Start with a wide "V" shape

2. Thicken the "V" and close the sides with angled lines

3. Add "shark fin" shape at head and triangle tail

4. Fill in solid and add feather details

CVH

DRAW A PITBULL

KNOW:
Simple shapes combined together can create more complex objects

UNDERSTAND:
Every complex object can be simplified into a series of connected geometrical and organic shapes

DO:
Create an original artwork of a pitbull dog. Use contour lines and shading to indicate muscle striations. Shade.

VOCABULARY:
Complex - A way of combining the elements of art in involved ways, to create intricate and complicated relationships. A picture composed of many shapes of different colors, sizes, and textures would be called complex.
Contour lines - The outline and other visible edges of a mass, figure or object

Draw a Pitbull Dog

MR. WOOFERS

1. Start with . . .

a small circle

over a slightly larger oval

2. Connect with neck lines

add bump

3. Add pointy ears and legs

thicker at top

bend here

4. Erase dotted areas

add mouth

Add feet

5. Add hind quarters

angled oval

bend leg

add back and belly

6. Add more details . . .

ear crease

erase dotted areas

add leg

7.

add muscle lines in leg

add another leg

8.

nose

lip bump

muscle bump

muscle ripple

tail

9.

draw toes with claws

lightly shade areas with muscle lines

CVH

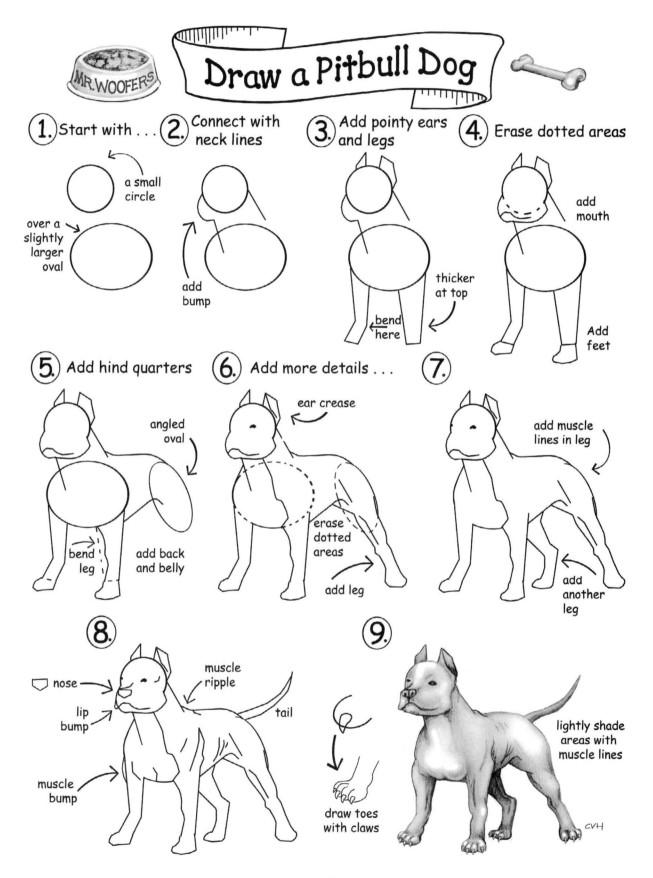

IN THE DOGHOUSE

KNOW:
Simple steps to create a ¾ view of a house

UNDERSTAND:
One way to create the appearance of a 3D house showing perspective at a ¾ view

DO:
Create an original paneled doghouse in a landscape scene showing perspective. Add a dog of your choice and shade.

VOCABULARY:
Landscape - An artwork which depicts scenery. There is usually some sky in the scene.
Perspective - The illusion of 3D on a 2D surface, creating a sense of depth and receding space
Three-Quarter (3/4) View - A view of a face or any other subject which is half-way between a full and a side view

In The Doghouse

1. Start with three vertical lines

2. Connect them at the top and bottom

← straight line →

← angled →

3. Draw an arrow pointing upward

overlaps here

doesn't touch

4. Add "thickness" to the roof

receding lines

5.

erase dotted area

angled boards

6. Add a dog and shade

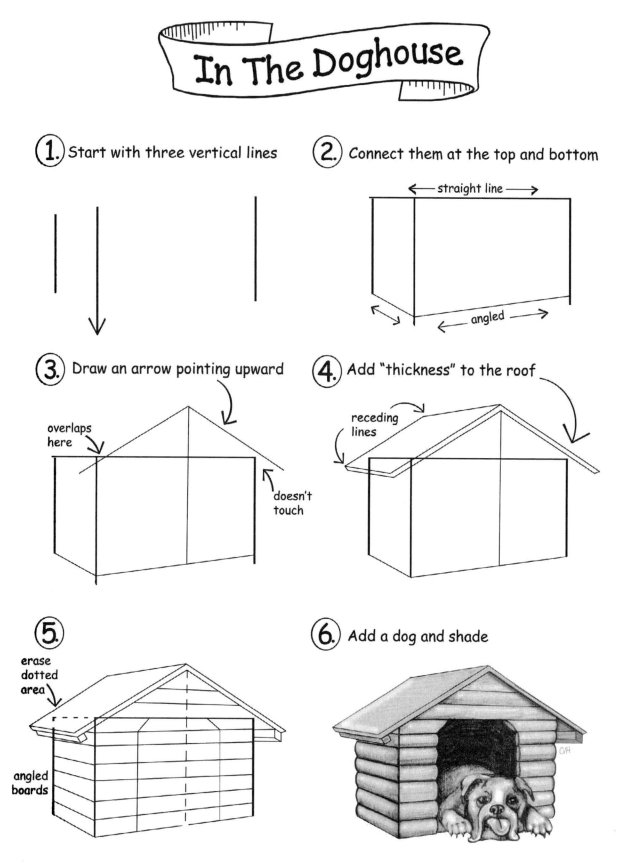

155

LION HEAD

KNOW:
The steps to create a lion head

UNDERSTAND:
• A simple grid can aid in the drawing of a proportionate lion face
• The techniques an artist uses to show how something might feel or what it is made of in an artwork

DO:
Practice drawing a lion head using the steps provided. Indicate texture on the mane with a series of curving lines. Shade.

VOCABULARY:
Grid - A framework or pattern of criss-crossed or parallel lines that can be used as guidelines for placement of drawn objects
Proportion - the comparative sizes and placement of one part to another
Texture - The way something looks like it might feel like in an artwork

Draw a Lion Head

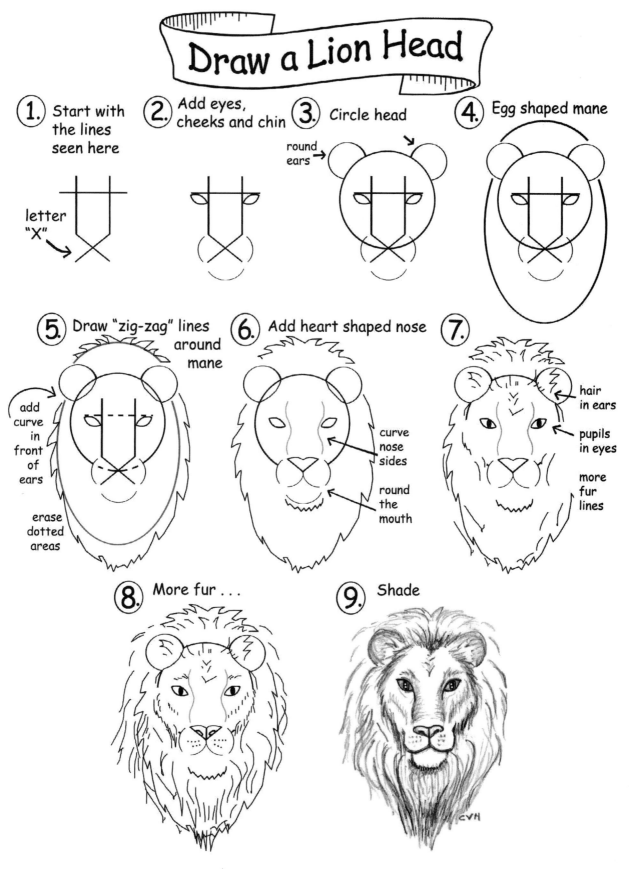

1. Start with the lines seen here

letter "X"

2. Add eyes, cheeks and chin

3. Circle head

round ears →

4. Egg shaped mane

5. Draw "zig-zag" lines around mane

add curve in front of ears

erase dotted areas

6. Add heart shaped nose

curve nose sides

round the mouth

7.

hair in ears

pupils in eyes

more fur lines

8. More fur . . .

9. Shade

CVH

COW SKULL

KNOW:
Simple shapes combined together can create more complex objects

UNDERSTAND:
Combining simple shapes in layers, connecting them with lines and erasing the insides is a trick used by artists to create a likeness

DO:
• Practice breaking down objects into simple shapes by looking around the room at items and visually simplifying them
• Follow the steps provided and create your own version of a cow skull

VOCABULARY:
Combine - Two or more objects put together
Layer - Something placed over another surface

Draw a Cow Skull

1. Start with a circle

2. Add an oval — overlap

3. Add a rectangle — skinny and long

4. Erase inside

5. Add small squares — chop corners here and here

6. Connect outer rim — connect

7. Erase insides

8. Add squares — triangle eye shape

9. Add curved horns — round all corner points — 1/2 circle in eye — add nostrils using a "W" shape

10. Shade and add "extra's" like cracks or barbed wire

Mooo!

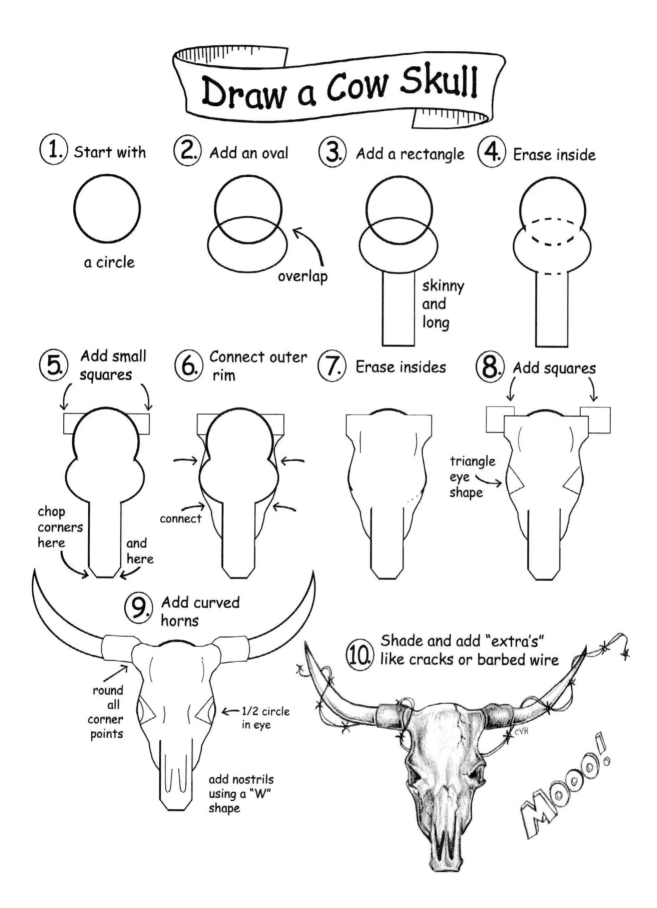

CVH

DRAW A COBRA

KNOW:
Simple shapes combined together can create more complex objects

UNDERSTAND:
Adding contour lines by "wrapping" them around tubes gives the appearance of detail and 3D

DO:
• Follow the steps provided and create your own version of a coiled cobra snake
• Shade

VOCABULARY:
Contour Lines - The outline or inner detail lines of an object that show form
Volume - Refers to the space within a form

Draw a Cobra

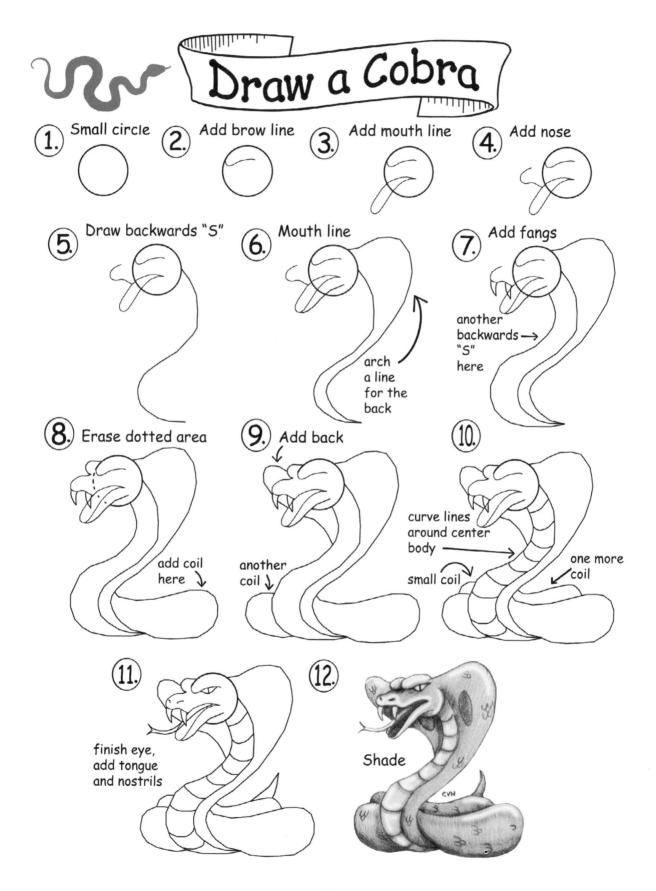

1. Small circle

2. Add brow line

3. Add mouth line

4. Add nose

5. Draw backwards "S"

6. Mouth line

arch a line for the back

7. Add fangs

another backwards → "S" here

8. Erase dotted area

add coil here ↓

9. Add back

another coil ↓

10.

curve lines around center body →

small coil

one more coil

11. finish eye, add tongue and nostrils

12. Shade

CVH

CLIMBING TIGER

KNOW:
• Overlapping, Layering, Pattern

UNDERSTAND:
Layering simple shapes can be the first step to creating complex forms

DO:
Follow the steps provided to create a climbing tiger. Make it unique by creating an original stripe pattern that "wraps" around it's body. The "wrapping" indicates form. Shade.

VOCABULARY:
Layering - To place something over another surface or object
Overlapping - When one thing lies over and partly covers something else
Pattern - The repetition of shapes, lines or colors in a design

Climbing Tiger

1. Start with 2 overlapping ovals

angled diagonally ←

2. Add 4 smaller ovals for limbs

3. Erase areas as seen below

4. Add 2 circle paws, 1 head and 2 oval lower legs

connect neck ←

5. Add ear, nose and chin shapes, 2 feet and tail

6. Erase as seen below.

"Thicken" tail

7. Claws & facial features

8. "Wrap" stripes around the body

9. Stripes on legs

10. Shade

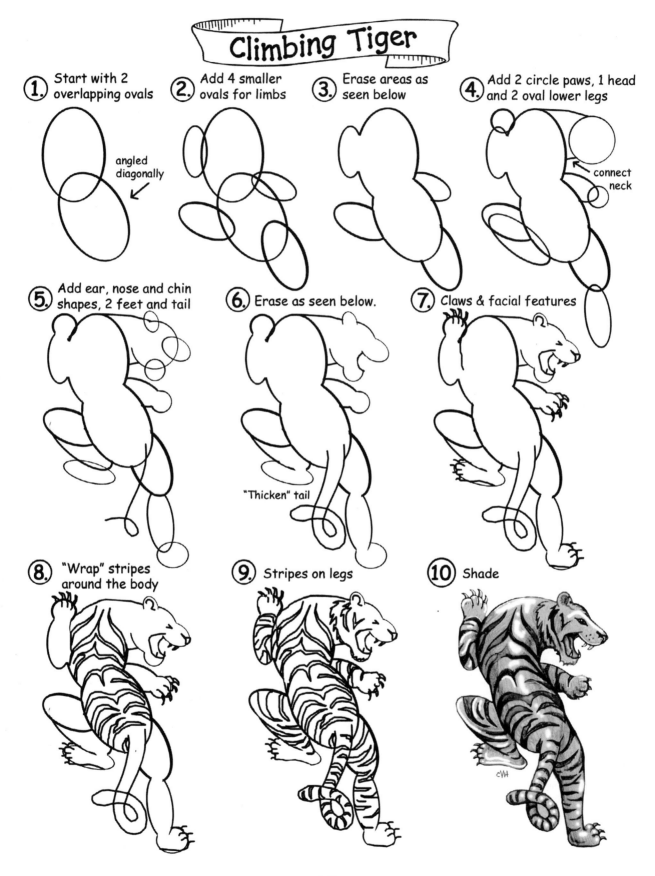

CVH

DRAGON

KNOW:
Contour Lines, Overlapping, Pattern, Stylize

UNDERSTAND:
How to start with a simple spiral line and build on it until it becomes a unique artwork representing a dragon

DO:
- Follow the steps provided to create a stylized dragon
- Use pattern and contour lines to show detail and form
- Shade

VOCABULARY:
Contour Lines - The outline or inner detail lines of an object that show form
Overlapping - When one thing lies over and partly covers something else
Pattern - The repetition of shapes, lines or colors in a design
Stylize - To alter natural shapes, forms, colors, or textures in order to make a representation in a preset style or manner, rather than according to nature or tradition

Dragon from the Orient

1. Start with a curvy line

2. Double the line thickness

3. Add a mouth and circle head

4. Add "horns" and brow — and feet

5. Draw spines on back, claws and belly ridges

6. Add fang and spine details

7. More detail

8. Shade

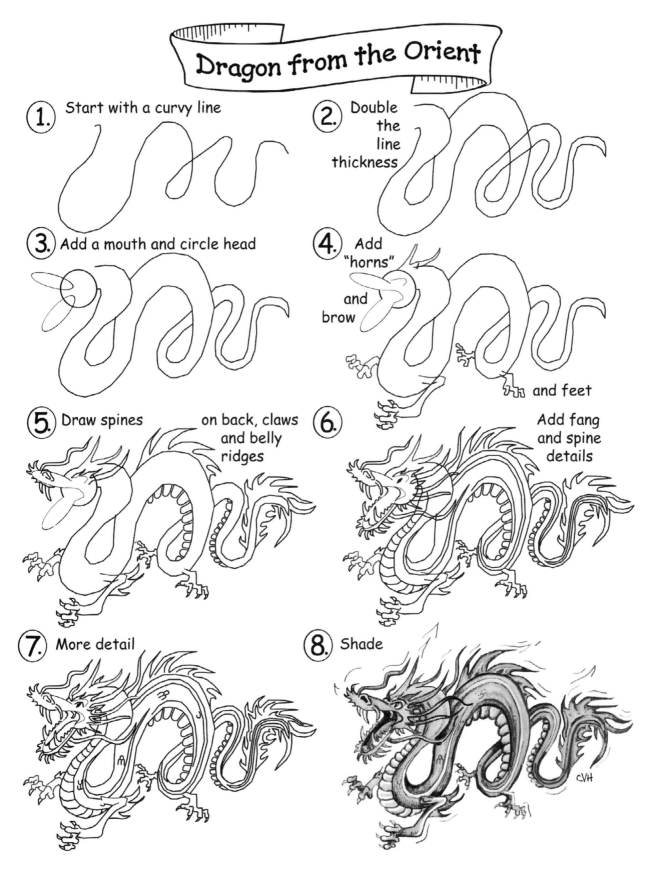

CVH

Chapter 6

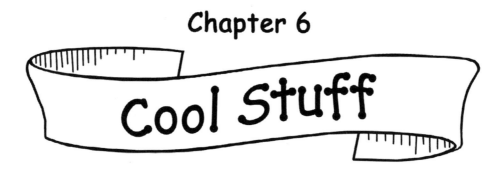

Cool Stuff

PRAYING HANDS

KNOW:
• Symmetry an Organic Shape

UNDERSTAND:
• How to represent realistic praying hands using contour lines, shading and small details
• How to break down organic forms into simple, angular lines

DO:
Create a realistic set of praying hands following the steps provided. Add "extra's" like Rosary beads, handcuffs, etc. to make it unique. Don't worry about trying to make the hands the same on both sides - things are rarely exactly symmetrical in nature. Shade.

VOCABULARY:
Contour Lines - The outline or inner detail lines of an object that show form
Organic Shape - An irregular shape that might be found in nature, rather than a mechanical or angular shape
Symmetry - An object that is the same on both sides

Praying Hands

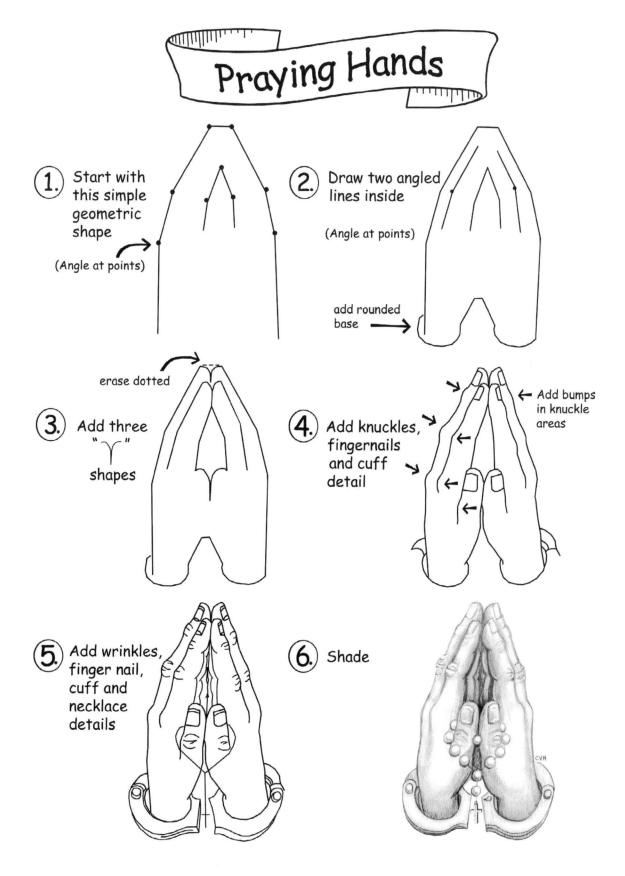

1. Start with this simple geometric shape

(Angle at points)

2. Draw two angled lines inside

(Angle at points)

add rounded base →

erase dotted

3. Add three " ⌄ " shapes

4. Add knuckles, fingernails and cuff detail

← Add bumps in knuckle areas

5. Add wrinkles, finger nail, cuff and necklace details

6. Shade

CVH

SKELETON HAND

KNOW:
Bones of the Hand, Contour line and Observation

UNDERSTAND:
Drawing a likeness through observation

DO:
Based on your own hand, draw a skeleton hand while learning the names of each bone section using the tips and tricks provided. As you draw, observe your hand and note where the knuckles are. These represent the sections between bones.

TIP: Hold your pencil at a 90 degree angle when tracing your hand.

VOCABULARY:
Contour - The outline and other visible edges of a mass, figure or object
Observation - Receiving knowledge of the outside world through the senses

TIP: This looks really cool when drawn on black construction paper using white oil pastels. Still use pencil for the outline of the hand. It's not as easy to see, but you don't need to erase it after for the skeleton hand effect.

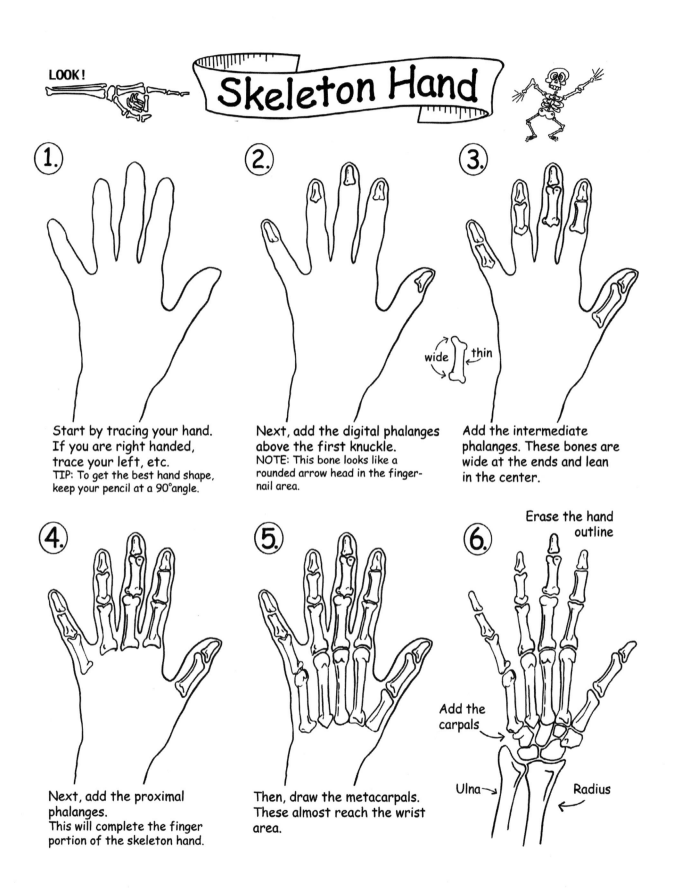

LOOK!

Skeleton Hand

1. Start by tracing your hand. If you are right handed, trace your left, etc.
TIP: To get the best hand shape, keep your pencil at a 90°angle.

2. Next, add the digital phalanges above the first knuckle.
NOTE: This bone looks like a rounded arrow head in the finger-nail area.

3. Add the intermediate phalanges. These bones are wide at the ends and lean in the center.

wide — thin

4. Next, add the proximal phalanges.
This will complete the finger portion of the skeleton hand.

5. Then, draw the metacarpals. These almost reach the wrist area.

6. Erase the hand outline

Add the carpals

Ulna →

Radius

THREE SKULLS

KNOW:
• Mirror Symmetry/Balance
• Major bones of the head

UNDERSTAND:
• The basics of proportion to create a skull
• Mirror symmetry is when the parts of an image or object are organized so that one side duplicates (mirrors) the other
• Perfect symmetry is rarely found in nature
• Complex forms can be simplified into shapes

DO:
Student will discuss the major bones of the head and the basic proportions of a human skull. They will then create an original artwork of "Three Skulls" using simple geometric shapes embellished into complex forms and indicate mirror symmetry.

VOCABULARY:
Balance - The way the elements of art are arranged to create a feeling of stability in a work; a pleasing or harmonious arrangement of parts in a design or composition
Cranium - Portion of the skull that encloses the braincase
Human Skull - Supports face structures and forms a cavity for the brain
Mandible - The lower jawbone
Mirror Symmetry - The parts of an image or object organized so that one side duplicates (or mirrors) the other
Proportion - The comparative sizes and placement of one part to another

Three Skulls

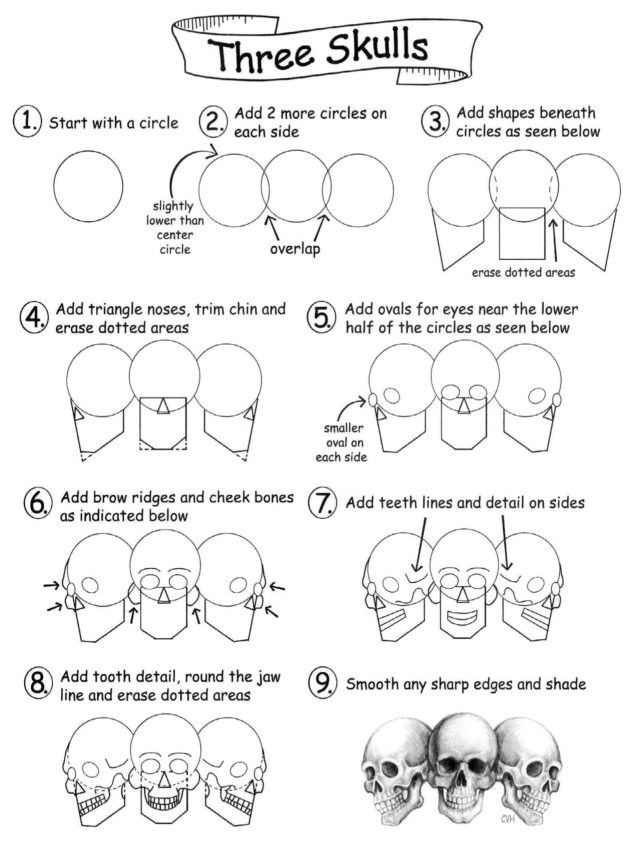

1. Start with a circle

2. Add 2 more circles on each side

slightly lower than center circle

overlap

3. Add shapes beneath circles as seen below

erase dotted areas

4. Add triangle noses, trim chin and erase dotted areas

5. Add ovals for eyes near the lower half of the circles as seen below

smaller oval on each side

6. Add brow ridges and cheek bones as indicated below

7. Add teeth lines and detail on sides

8. Add tooth detail, round the jaw line and erase dotted areas

9. Smooth any sharp edges and shade

CVH

HAND POSITIONS
(Pointing Finger)

KNOW:
Foreshortening, Perspective

UNDERSTAND:
How to create the illusion of 3D in which the sizes of near and far parts of an object contrast greatly

DO:
Create an original drawing of a pointing hand as viewed from straight on. Make sure the pointing finger is much larger than the rest of the hand in order to give the appearance of foreshortening. Don't trace. Shade.

TIPS: When shading, make the darkest values between the fingers and knuckle creases. Erase some spots on the upper knuckles, finger centers and between the creases to create a natural highlight effect.

VOCABULARY:
Foreshortening - A way of representing an object so that it conveys the illusion of depth, seeming to thrust forward or go back into space. Foreshortening's success often depends upon a point of view or perspective in which the sizes of near and far parts of a subject contrast greatly.

Highlight - The area on any surface which reflects the most light; to direct attention to or emphasize an area of a drawing through use of value

Perspective - The technique used create a sense of depth or receding space in an art work; the illusion of 3D onto a 2D surface

Point of View - A position or angle from which something is observed or considered; the direction of the viewer's gaze

Hand Positions
Pointing at You

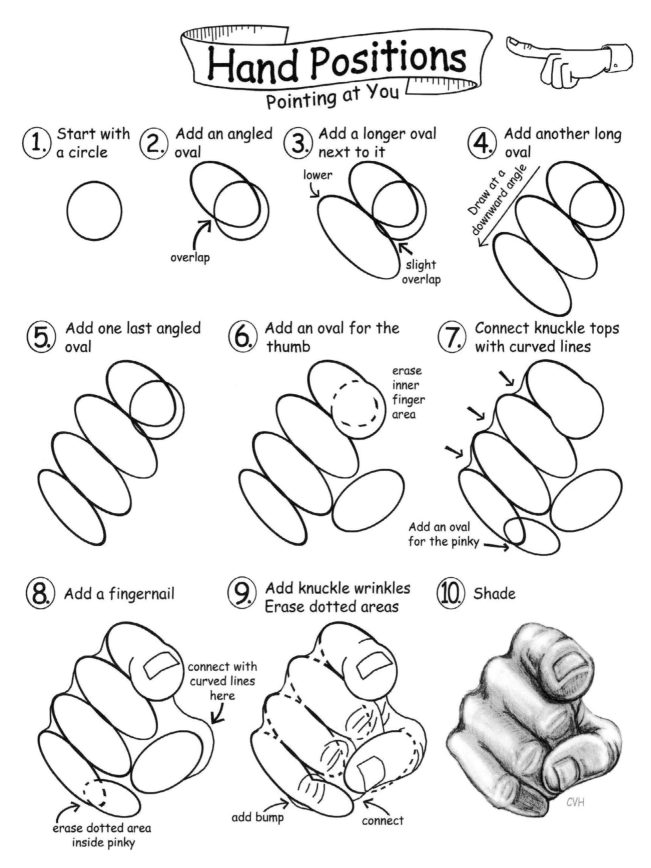

1. Start with a circle

2. Add an angled oval
   overlap

3. Add a longer oval next to it
   lower
   slight overlap

4. Add another long oval
   Draw at a downward angle

5. Add one last angled oval

6. Add an oval for the thumb
   erase inner finger area

7. Connect knuckle tops with curved lines
   Add an oval for the pinky

8. Add a fingernail
   connect with curved lines here
   erase dotted area inside pinky

9. Add knuckle wrinkles Erase dotted areas
   add bump
   connect

10. Shade

CVH

175

HAND POSITIONS
(Holding a Melting Clock)

KNOW:
Perspective, Proportion

UNDERSTAND:
• The use of proportion, perspective and observation to create a hand holding an object
• Subtle differences in shape and size make our hands unique

DO:
Create an original drawing of a human hand holding an object (melting clock). Start with a series of "fanned out" ovals and build on those shapes, eventually turning them into finger forms. View your own cupped hand and observe the natural sizing and angles for reference. Don't trace. Shade.

VOCABULARY:
Form - A 3D shape (height, width, and depth) that encloses volume

Highlight - The area on any surface which reflects the most light; to direct attention to or emphasize an area of a drawing through use of value

Perspective - The technique artists use to project an illusion of the three-dimensional world onto a two-dimensional surface. Perspective helps to create a sense of depth and receding space.

Proportion - A principle of design, proportion refers to the comparative, relationship of one part of an object to another

Extensions:
In 1931, Salvador Dalí painted one of his most famous works, The Persistence of Memory, which introduced a surrealistic image of soft, melting pocket watches.

The Persistence of Memory is famous painting of melting clocks made in 1931 by Salvador Dali.

Hand Positions
Holding Items

1. Draw an angled oval

2. Add another

Draw light guidelines to help with finger placement

slightly lower

3. and another slightly smaller here

higher

4. Add a pinky

5. Add a thumb

6. Erase guides. Add nails.

7. Add "wrinkles" at knuckle area

8. Add circle shape in palm area for clock

9. Draw extentions to each finger & "melting" drips

dent

10. Add clock face. Shade

CVH

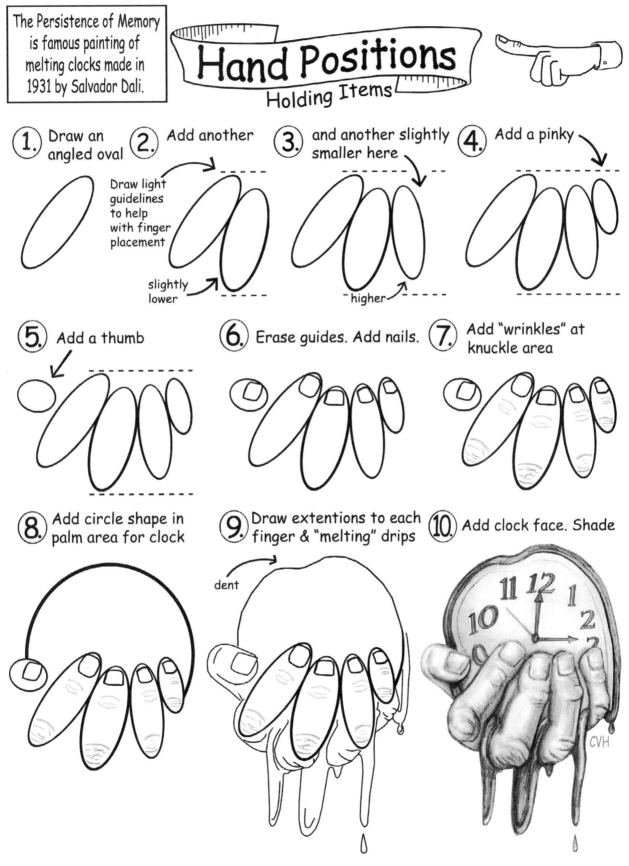

POCKET WATCH

KNOW:
Angle, Balance, Pattern, Perspective, Repetition, Roman Numerals

UNDERSTAND:
Placing simple geometric shapes in a specific pattern or at an angle can add to the realism and detail of an object as well as create interest and the illusion of depth.

DO:
• Follow the steps provided to create a detailed "open" stopwatch based on simple geometric shape guidelines
• Using numbers or Roman Numerals, balance those numbers equally and in sequence around the clock face (i.e. #12 is 180 degrees from the #6)
• Use learned 3D techniques which concentrate on perspective to convey the illusion of depth. Students will also consider size, position, detail and hue.

VOCABULARY:
Angle - The figure formed by two planes diverging from a common line. "Angle" can refer to the space between such lines or surfaces, and it can also refer to a direction or point of view.

Perspective - The technique used to create the illusion of 3D onto a 2D surface. Perspective helps to create a sense of depth or receding space.

Roman Numerals - The numeric system in ancient Rome, uses combinations of letters from the Latin alphabet to signify values

Pocket Watch

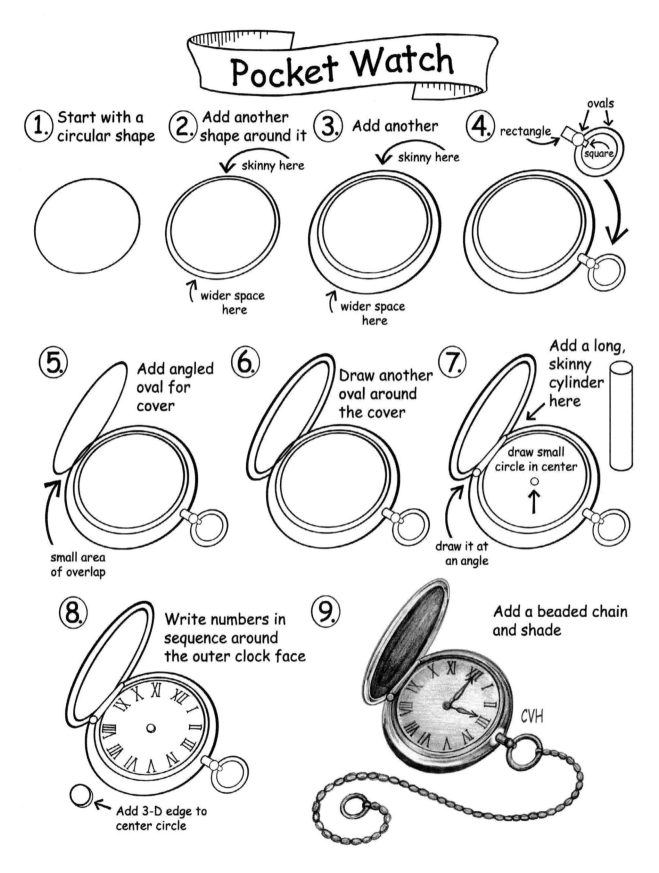

1. Start with a circular shape

2. Add another shape around it
   - skinny here
   - wider space here

3. Add another
   - skinny here
   - wider space here

4. rectangle — ovals — square

5. Add angled oval for cover
   - small area of overlap

6. Draw another oval around the cover

7. Add a long, skinny cylinder here
   - draw small circle in center
   - draw it at an angle

8. Write numbers in sequence around the outer clock face
   - Add 3-D edge to center circle

9. Add a beaded chain and shade

CVH

CHAIN LINKS

KNOW:
Overlapping

UNDERSTAND:
How to create the appearance of interlocking forms by using overlapping techniques and shading

DO:
• Create a realistic chain of interlocking links using the tips and tricks provided
• Shade
• Erase some areas on each link to create a metallic "shine" effect

VOCABULARY:
Overlapping - When one thing lies over and partly covers something else

Chain Links

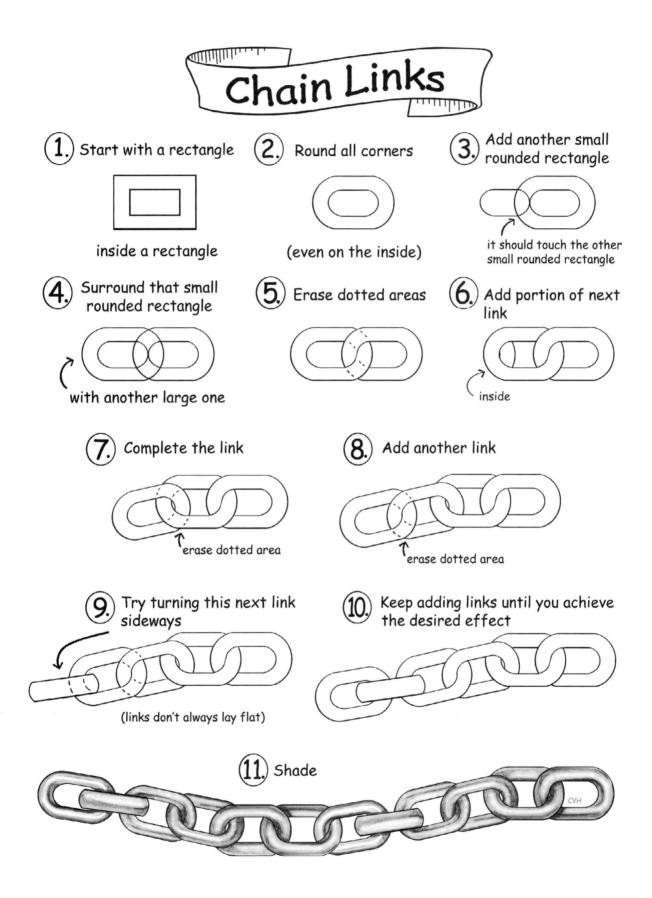

1. Start with a rectangle

inside a rectangle

2. Round all corners

(even on the inside)

3. Add another small rounded rectangle

it should touch the other small rounded rectangle

4. Surround that small rounded rectangle

with another large one

5. Erase dotted areas

6. Add portion of next link

inside

7. Complete the link

erase dotted area

8. Add another link

erase dotted area

9. Try turning this next link sideways

(links don't always lay flat)

10. Keep adding links until you achieve the desired effect

11. Shade

CVH

181

COMPASS ROSE

KNOW:
Balance, Compass, Repetition, Rotational Symmetry

UNDERSTAND:
• How to arrange elements in an artwork so that they appear symmetrical or equally balanced
• A compass rose is used to display the orientation of the cardinal directions and their intermediate points

DO:
• Follow the steps provided to create an original Compass Rose design focusing on rotational symmetry
• Shade with pencil or color with marker

VOCABULARY:
Balance - A principle of design, balance refers to the way the elements of art are arranged to create a feeling of stability in a work; a pleasing or harmonious arrangement or proportion of parts or areas in a design or composition.

Compass - A navigational instrument that measures directions in a frame of reference that is stationary relative to the surface of the earth. The frame of reference defines the four cardinal directions (or points) - north, south, east, and west.

Compass Rose - (Sometimes called a Windrose) is a figure on a compass, map, nautical chart or monument used to display the orientation of the cardinal directions and their intermediate points

Rotational Symmetry - An object that looks the same after a certain amount of circular movement around that object's center

Symmetry - An object that is the same on both sides

Compass Rose

1. Use a ruler and draw a symmetrical cross

2. Draw an "X" shape through the cross

this will create 8 equal 45° angles

3. Place 4 dots at equal intervals on the "X" part

make a triangle using the top point of the cross and upper 2 dots

4. Draw a line from each dot to the nearest point of the first cross

5. Make another set of points up from the previous

make 2 points on each "triangle"

6. Draw a line from each dot to the nearest point of the second cross

7. Darken your lines with a thin marker and erase any extra pencil lines

8. Fill in the right side of each triangle with a dark color

9. Fill in the remaining blank areas with a lighter color

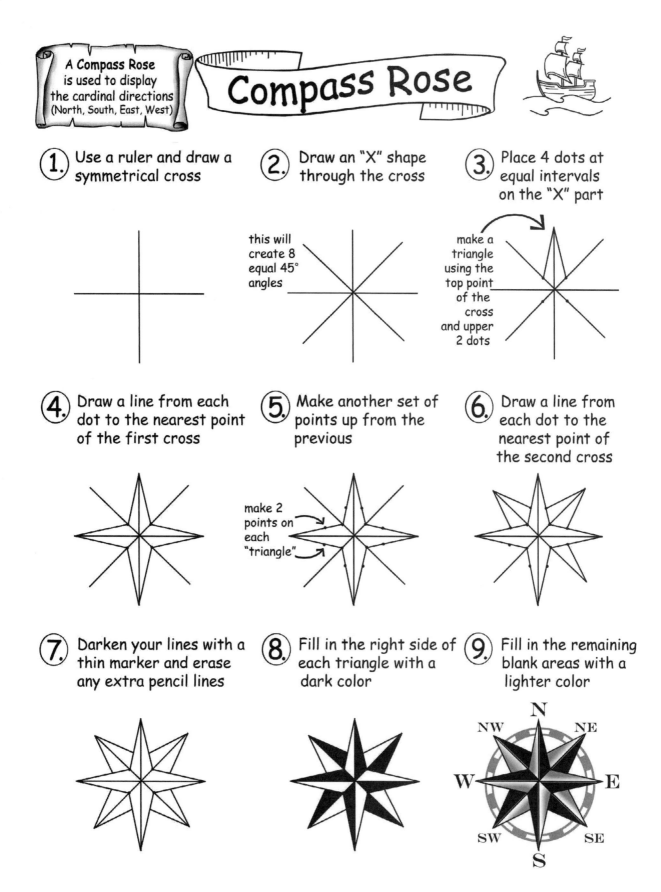

CUPCAKE TREATS

KNOW:
Balance, Ellipse, Repetition

UNDERSTAND:
• The difference between shape and form
• How to arrange elements in an artwork so that they appear symmetrical or equally balanced
• Ellipses in art can help give the appearance of a 3D object

DO:
• Follow the steps provided to create an original cupcake design that starts with simple shapes that are eventually connected to create complex forms
• Use learned 3D techniques which concentrate on overlapping to convey the illusion of depth. Students will also consider size, position, detail and color.

VOCABULARY:
Balance - A principle of design, balance refers to the way the elements of art are arranged to create a feeling of stability in a work; a pleasing or harmonious arrangement or proportion of parts or areas in a design or composition
Oval - (ellipse) A two-dimensional shape that looks like a circle that has been stretched to make it longer

Cupcake Treat

zigzag - line with short, sharp angles

1. Start with a skinny oval

2. Add slightly angled vertical lines on each side

angled inward

curved slightly

3. Curve a zigzag pattern around the original oval

4. Draw vertical lines coming from the zig-zag points

Erase the oval top (shown as dotted line)

5. Add a dollop of frosting

6. Define frosting edges

Top with a candy

Decorate and Shade

CVH

ALIEN SKULL

KNOW:
Geometric Shape, Angle

UNDERSTAND:
A simple circle can be the basic starting point for a variety of artistic creations

DO:
• Create your version of an alien skull using the tips and trick provided
• Shade outside rim darker than the inside for a 3D, rounded effect

VOCABULARY:
Angle - A figure formed by two lines or edges diverging from or crossing a common point
Geometric - Any shape or form having mathematic design. Geometric designs are typically made with straight lines or shapes from geometry.

Alien Skull

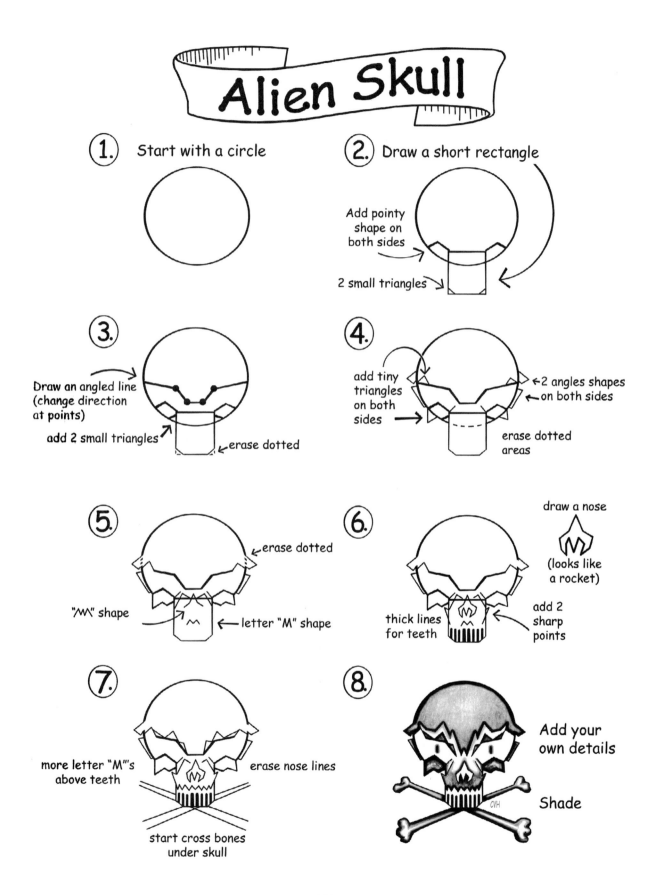

1. Start with a circle

2. Draw a short rectangle

Add pointy shape on both sides

2 small triangles

3. Draw an angled line (change direction at points)

add 2 small triangles

erase dotted

4. add tiny triangles on both sides

2 angles shapes on both sides

erase dotted areas

5. erase dotted

"/W\" shape

letter "M" shape

6. draw a nose

(looks like a rocket)

thick lines for teeth

add 2 sharp points

7. more letter "M"'s above teeth

erase nose lines

start cross bones under skull

8. Add your own details

Shade

GET ON THE MICROPHONE

KNOW:
Sphere, Cylinder, Rectangle, Pattern

UNDERSTAND:
Connecting shapes to create recognizable, everyday forms

DO:
• Choose a style and create your version of a microphone using the outline provided
• "Wrap" lines around the circle of the modern microphone to create a sphere. "Wrap" lines around the older style microphone to indicate angles and edges.
• Add pattern details and shade

VOCABULARY:
Cylinder - A tube that appears three dimensional
Pattern - The repetition of shapes, lines, or colors in a design
Sphere - A three-dimensional form shaped like a ball, circular from all possible points of view

Get on the Mic

① Start with a circle

② Add the base

③ Add curved lines to show form

④ Shade

2 angled lines

wider at top

curve the bottom

thinner towards bottom

follow the rounded shape for pattern

CVH

old-school

① Draw a tilted rectangle

② Round the corners

③ Add angled shapes as seen below

④ Add details and shade

add a square

add a line

erase dotted areas

CVH

189

GRAVES WITH DRAPERY

KNOW:
Drapery, Texture

UNDERSTAND:
• Creating complex forms from simple shapes
• Texture is used by artists to show how something might feel or what it is made of
• The study of ways to represent drapery is essential in the development of an artist's skills. Drapery folds are composed of curving surfaces reflecting gradations of value.

DO:
Create a cemetery scene or headstone memorial including at least 2 graves showing 3D edges, a "wood-look" texture and folds of fabric

VOCABULARY:
Drapery - Cloth or a representation of cloth arranged to hang in folds
Texture - The way something looks like it might feel like in an artwork. Simulated textures are suggested by an artist with different brushstrokes, pencil lines, etc.
Value - The lightness or darkness of a color

Graves with Drapery

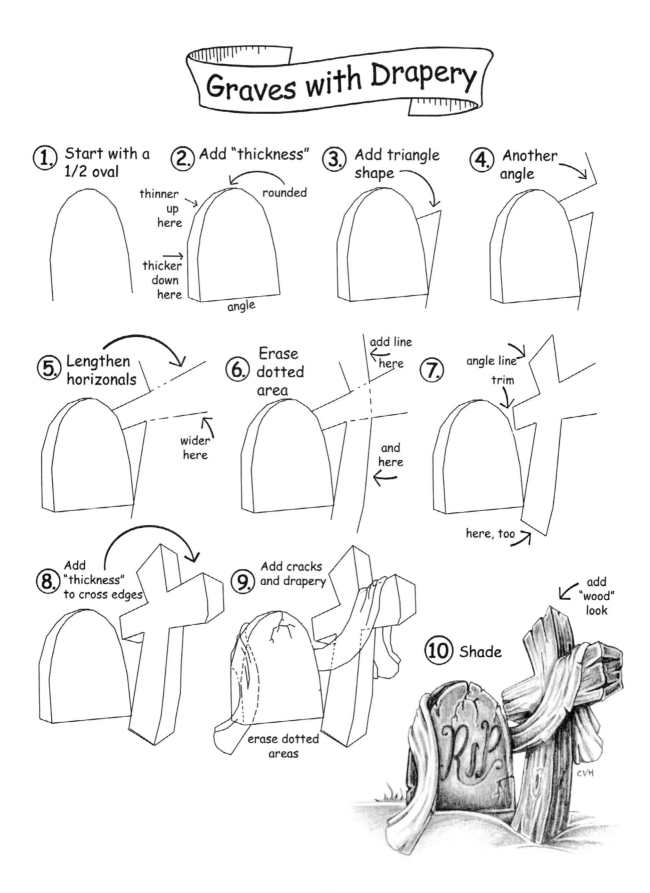

① Start with a 1/2 oval

② Add "thickness"

thinner up here

rounded

thicker down here

angle

③ Add triangle shape

④ Another angle

⑤ Lengthen horizonals

wider here

⑥ Erase dotted area

add line here

and here

⑦

angle line

trim

here, too

⑧ Add "thickness" to cross edges

⑨ Add cracks and drapery

erase dotted areas

⑩ Shade

add "wood" look

CVH

191

DRAW THE EARTH

KNOW:
Sphere, Continents, Curved lines

UNDERSTAND:
Lines and shapes drawn in a curved fashion on top of a circle help to create the illusion of a sphere

DO:
- Choose a view of the Earth to draw from the handout or a globe
- "Wrap" the continents around the circle
- Add details and shade

VOCABULARY:
Continents - The large landmasses on Earth with seven regions: Asia, Africa, North America, South America, Antarctica, Europe, and Australia
Sphere - A three-dimensional form shaped like a ball, circular from all possible points of view

Draw the Earth

This tutorial shows only two of the many views of our planet

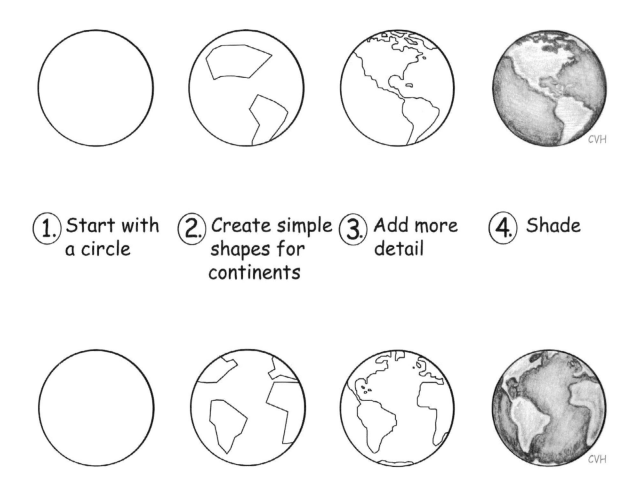

1. Start with a circle
2. Create simple shapes for continents
3. Add more detail
4. Shade

BIRD CAGE

KNOW:
The simple steps to create a 3D bird cage

UNDERSTAND:
• A transparent cylinder allows us to see through the form at all angles
• Lines that wrap around the top of the shape help to create the illusion of form

DO:
• Follow the steps provided to create a bird cage. Be sure to draw lines on the "front" and "back" to indicate the illusion of 3D
• Add "extra's" like a bird

VOCABULARY:
Cylinder - A tube that appears three dimensional
Ellipse - A circle viewed at an angle (drawn as an oval)
Transparent - See through

The Bird Cage

use a ruler!

1. Start with a rectangle rounded at the top

2. Add an oval inside near the bottom

3. Add a curved line to "thicken" the oval

4. Erase area under oval (see dotted area)

5. Add 2 more ovals

6. Add parallel lines curved near the top for bars

7. Add bars to the "far-end" of the cage

8. Add a decorative top and an open door

9. Add shading details and "extras"

195

PAWS AND CLAWS

KNOW:
The simple steps to create paw prints and ripping claws

UNDERSTAND:
• Simple shapes combined together can create recognizable forms
• Small details can create powerful effects in drawing

DO:
Follow the steps provided to create a paw print and a set of ripping claws

VOCABULARY:
Effect - A result or consequence of some action or process
Organic Shape - An irregular shape that might be found in nature, rather than a mechanical or angular shape
Vertical - The direction going straight up and down

Paws and Claws

Paws

1. Start with a wide egg shape

← narrow here

wider here

2. Add 2 lines

keep some space here

3. Draw | | diagonals

4. Round the edges

5. Add 2 more toes . . .

6. Add small, curved triangle shape for claws

Claws

make a raindrop shape

→

turn it upside down and curve it

1. Start with 4 curved claws

2. Draw a long triangle from each claw top

3. Shade

Darken inside each triangle

add jagged edges for a ripping effect

CVH

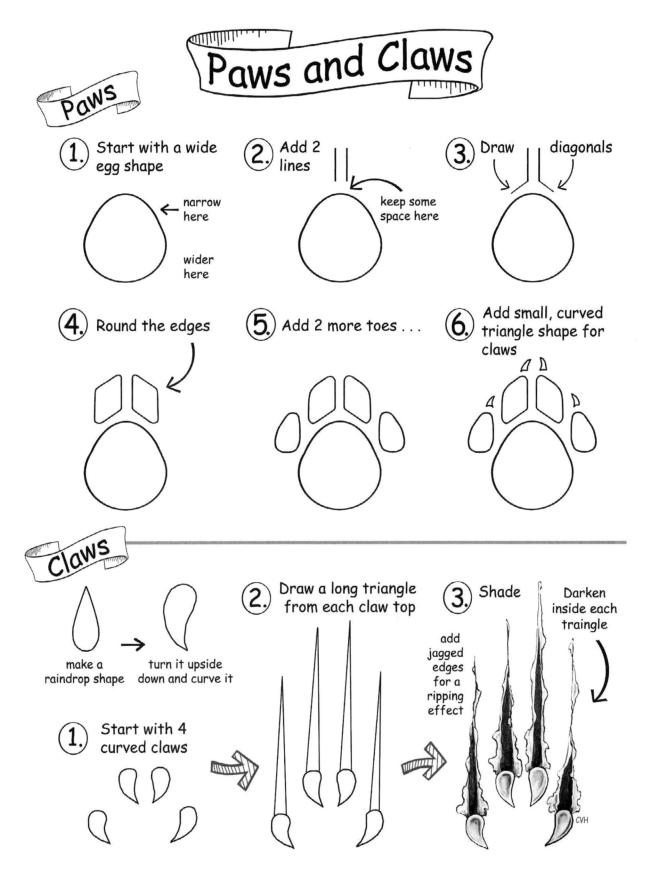

197

ANIME

KNOW:
Anime, Exaggerating Features, Caricature

UNDERSTAND:
• Characteristics of Anime art
• Use of exaggeration and distortion in an artwork to create a particular style

DO:
Follow the steps provided to create an original "Anime" style character

VOCABULARY:
Anime - Japanese style of animation, often exaggerating facial features on a character. The term is borrowed from the French word for animation and blends traditional Japanese woodblock style prints with American-style character design.

Caricature - A representation in which the subject's distinctive features or peculiarities are deliberately exaggerated to produce a comic or grotesque effect

Distortion - To change the way something looks — sometimes deforming or stretching an object or figure out of its normal shape to exaggerate the features

Exaggerate - Overstate, embellish; enlarge or shrink in size

Make Anything Anime

Draw lightly!

1. Start with a BIG head and a tiny body

2. "Thicken" the body

3. extra long hair on girls — giant eyes with "shiny" spots — tiny nose and mouth

3/4 view

1.

2. dent

3.

this works on animals, too!

DEXTER

Different Types of Eyes

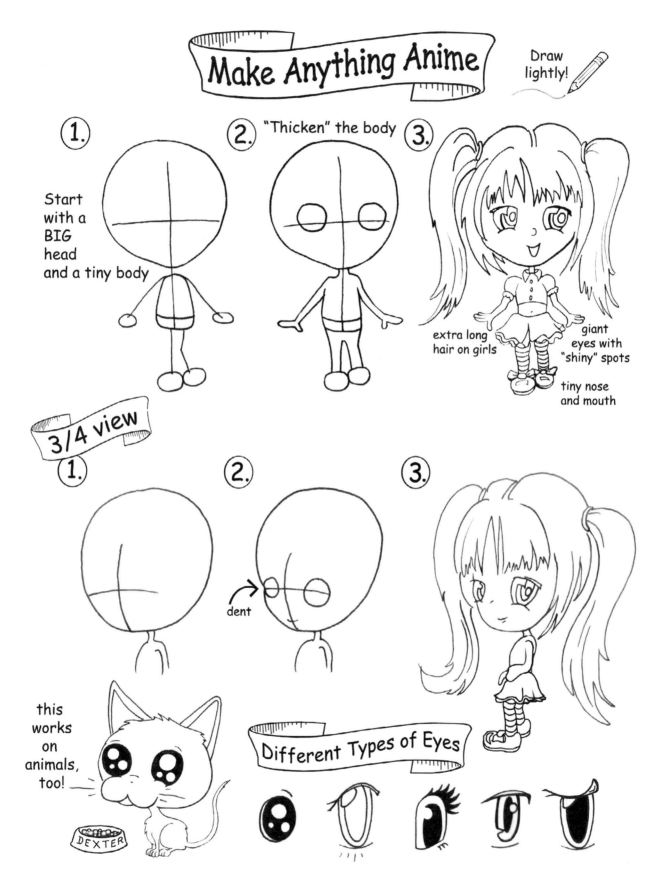

Anime Boy
3/4 face view

夢 dream
和 harmony

1. Start with a **BIG** head

face ← guide lines

and a smaller stick body with short legs and oval feet

← angled shoulder line

← hip line

↳ oval feet

2. Add to body

← cross arms

← rectangle hips

3. "Thicken" torso and legs

add eyes

← connect arms & hips

4. "Thicken" arms and upper body

add iris line in each eye and a tiny nose

5. Erase center guidelines

"shiny" eye circle

← "popped" collar

← untucked shirt

← cuff pants

6. Erase bottom guides. Add spiky hair-do.

add oval pupils

← pockets

more >

Anime Boy
finishing touches

7. Erase head and shirt guide lines

add another "shiny" eye circle

add buttons and logo on shirt

little wrinkle

8. Add details

hair highlights

shade pupils black and put "spike" lines in the iris

wallet chain

stitches in jeans

"shiny" spots on shoes

cVH

Anime Girl
3/4 face view

grace
happy

1. Start with a **BIG** head

face guide lines →

and a smaller stick body with short legs and oval feet

← angled shoulder line

← hip line

← oval feet

2. Add to body

add eye shape

add stick arms and oval hands

3. "Thicken" torso and add skirt shape

← add iris lines

← curve the base

4. "Thicken" arms and add a shirt

erase eye guide-lines

add thumb

add oval pupil

add ruffle to skirt

5. Add nose, mouth and hair "buns"

6. Erase center guides. Add hair.

add a tie

more >

Anime Girl
finishing touches

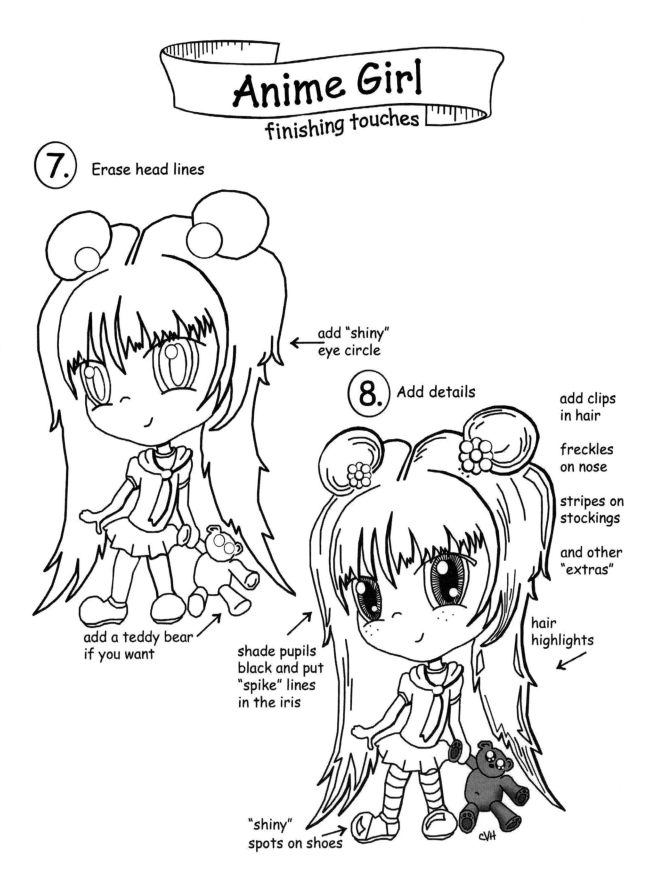

7. Erase head lines

← add "shiny" eye circle

8. Add details

add clips in hair

freckles on nose

stripes on stockings

and other "extras"

hair highlights

add a teddy bear if you want

shade pupils black and put "spike" lines in the iris

"shiny" spots on shoes

CVH

DRAW A LACE-UP CORSET

KNOW:
Overlapping

UNDERSTAND:
How to create the illusion of layers so that parts of a drawing appear to be in front of, or behind other parts

DO:
• Discuss examples of two-dimensional images which have near and far elements, focusing on how overlap and differences in size help to achieve an illusion of depth
• Follow the steps in the handout to create the look of layered/overlapping laces. The overlapping and size differences will show perspective. Students will indicate which parts of their picture appear to be on top and which parts appear to be on the bottom.

VOCABULARY:
Overlap - When one thing lies over and partly covers something else
Perspective - The point in which an object or scene is viewed

Lace-Up Corset

1. Start with a "V" shape open at the bottom

2. Add 1/2 ovals on each side for "hooks"

3. Erase "V" guide lines Add zig-zag as seen

4. Add zig-zag to opposite side creating curved "X" shapes

5. "Thicken" the laces by adding another line to each "X"

6. Erase ceratin lines so it looks like some laces are overlapping others

7. Add a bow

8. Erase area behind the bow

9. Shade

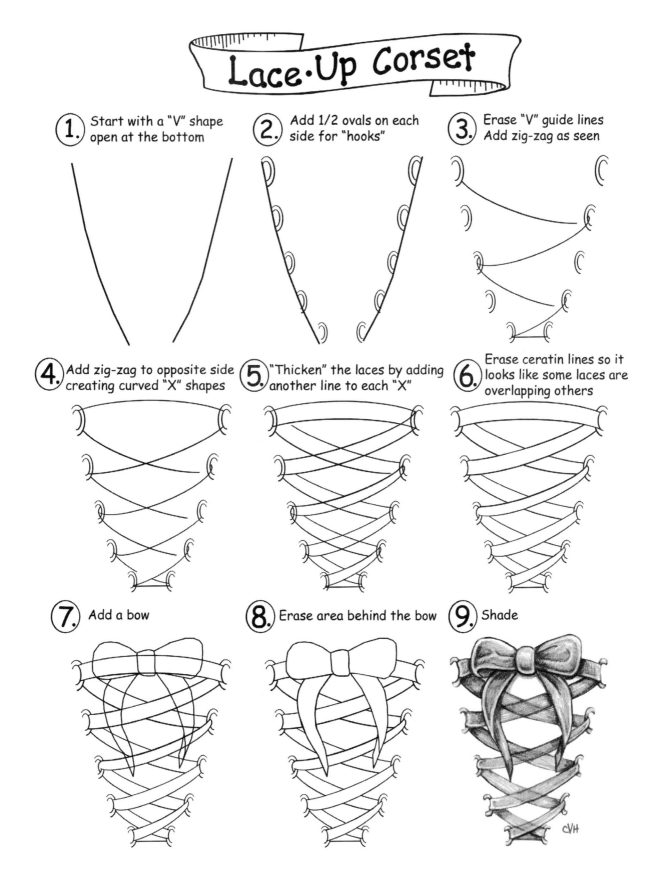

CVH

205

A FANCY TEA CUP

KNOW:
• Simple shapes combined create complex objects
• Cross section on a cone can create the illusion of a vessel (tea cup)
• Adding pattern and shading to an object give it form and dimension

UNDERSTAND:
• Using the principles of a cylinder (rounded base and an ellipse top) to create an object that appears to hold volume
• The technique of "wrapping" lines and pattern around an object so that it appears to have form

DO:
Create an original artwork of a tea cup and saucer that shows overlapping. Add "extra's" like a teabag or spoon and shade.

VOCABULARY:
Cone - Two lines at the edge of an ellipse that eventually meet
Ellipse - A circle viewed at an angle (drawn as an oval)
Overlap - When one thing lies over another, partially covering it
Volume - Refers to the space within a form

A Fancy Tea Cup

1. Start with a long, thin oval

2. Add 2 angled vertical lines

3. Round the bottom

4. Add curve to both sides

erase dotted areas

5. Add two ovals

one here

bigger one here for saucer

6.

erase dotted

add thickness to rim

7.

Add "thickness" to rim

use oval to make a fancy handle

erase dotted

Add slight curve for saucer base

8. Add a fancy design like flowers or swirls

Shade

CVH

SNEAKER DESIGN

KNOW:
Balance, Design, Function, Line, Repetition

UNDERSTAND:
• How fashion can create and divide social structures
• Fashion can reflect identity and be an extension of one's personality
• How to create an original design out of an existing structure

DO:
From conceptualization to final product, students will create a shoe design. Consider industry trends, design concepts, pattern, materials, color, line, symmetry, the wearer's personality, gender, age, likes/dislikes etc. when designing the shoe.

Don't forget: The purpose of the shoe (sports, casual wear, etc.), shoe shape (high top, low, etc.), stitching, reinforced areas, logos, laces/straps/velcro closure, grommets, sole texture, hang tags, etc.

PRESENTATION & REFLECTION:
You will need to include an artist statement/self reflection with your piece. In paragraph form, please include the following information as well as key vocabulary used in class.

    1. Describe your shoe design and your inspirations. What identity are you trying to convey? (Who are the shoes intended for? etc.)
    2. What areas have been easy or challenging in the design process?
    3. Describe the strengths and weaknesses in your shoe design.
    4. If you had to repeat this project, what would you do differently and why?

Shoes are much more than just functional clothing

Sneaker Design

Task: Create an original sneaker design. Brainstorm your concept using the ideas below

1.
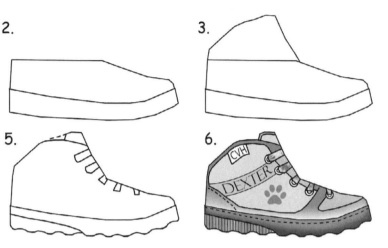

2.

3.

4.

5.

6.

Some Generic Sneaker Shapes

What do your shoes say about you?

1. Think about design elements that you like and make a list. It can include words, fonts, doodles, patterns, etc.

2. Decide what elements you want to include in your design. (line, font, text, graffiti, etc.)

3. Decide what identity you are trying to convey. Who are the shoes intended for?

Art Considerations:

industry trends
pattern
materials
color
balance
line
symmetry

Don't forget:

purpose of shoe
shoe shape
stitching
logo (endorsement?)
laces/straps
grommets
sole texture

TREASURE CHEST

KNOW:
• Simple shapes combined create complex objects
• Adding pattern and shading to an object give it form and dimension

UNDERSTAND:
• Using the principles of a cube to create an object that appears to hold volume
• The use of receding lines to show perspective
• One method to create a simple 3D cube

DO:
Create an original artwork of a treasure chest that demonstrates perspective. Add lots of "extra's" inside the chest. Put it in a scene.

VOCABULARY:
Cube - A polyhedron having six square faces; a square that appears 3D
Perspective - The point from which an object or scene is viewed
Receding Lines - Lines that move back or away from the foreground

Treasure Chest

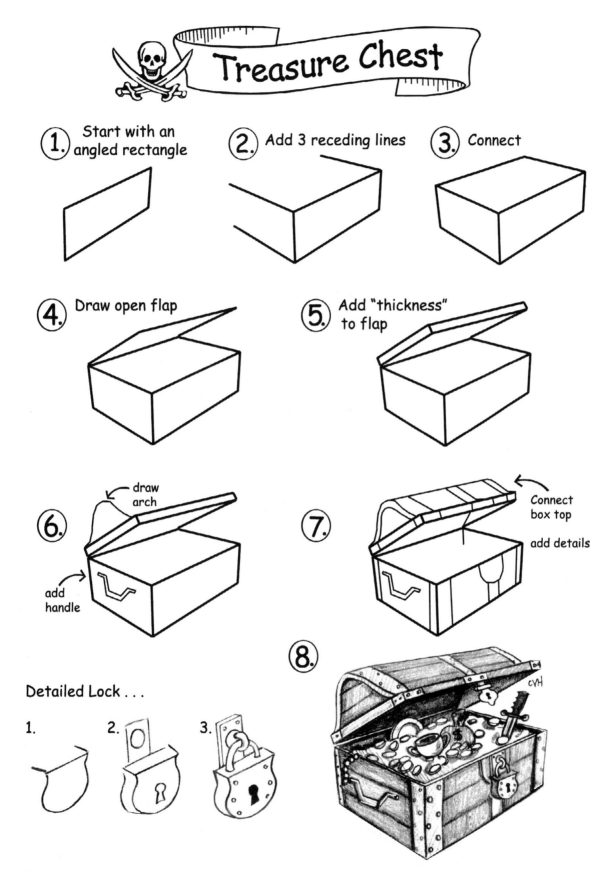

1. Start with an angled rectangle

2. Add 3 receding lines

3. Connect

4. Draw open flap

5. Add "thickness" to flap

6. draw arch
   add handle

7. Connect box top
   add details

8.

Detailed Lock . . .

1.   2.   3.

SKELETON PIRATE

KNOW:
Geometric Shapes, Overlapping and Layering

UNDERSTAND:
• Layering simple shapes can be the first step to creating complex forms
• The average human body can measured as "7 heads high"

DO:
• Follow the steps provided to create your own version of a unique "Skeleton" Pirate
• Add lots of "extra's" like a treasure chest, pirate ship, or scroll treasure map
• Put him in a scene and shade

VOCABULARY:
Geometric - Any shape or form having mathematical design. Geometric designs are typically made with straight lines or shapes from geometry (as opposed to organic, free-form lines)

Layering - To place something over another surface or objects
Overlapping - When one thing lies over and partly covers something else

Draw a Skeleton Pirate

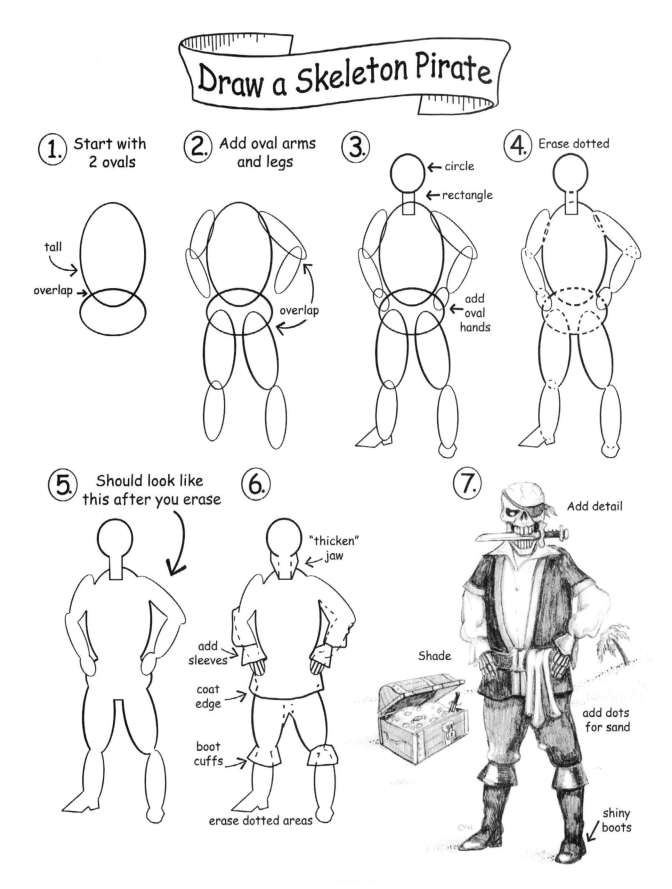

1. Start with 2 ovals

tall
overlap

2. Add oval arms and legs

overlap

3. ← circle
← rectangle

add oval hands →

4. Erase dotted

5. Should look like this after you erase

6. "thicken" jaw ←

add sleeves
coat edge →
boot cuffs →

erase dotted areas

7.

Add detail

Shade

add dots for sand

shiny boots ↓

WOODEN CROSS

KNOW:
Texture

UNDERSTAND:
• Creating complex forms from simple shapes
• Texture is used by artists to show how something might feel or what it is **made of**

DO:
Create an original cross that includes a "wood-look" texture and shows perspective

VOCABULARY:
Perspective - The point from which an object or scene is viewed
Texture - The way something looks like it might feel like in an artwork. Simulated textures are suggested by an artist with different brushstrokes, pencil lines, etc.
Value - The lightness or darkness of a color
Vertical - Parallel lines that are drawn straight up and down

A Wooden Cross

1. Start with 2 vertical lines

close with angled lines at top and bottom

2. Add 2 horizontal lines for a lower case "t"

← angle it →

3. Draw 7 short angled lines

one at each corner

4. Connect lines to give the illusion of 3-D

5. Add 2 parallel angled lines

one in back

one in front

6. Connect the lines to create the base

7. Add 2 "∨" shapes for base

8. Close the base with vertical lines

9. Shade with "wood look"

WOOD SAMPLE

a bunch of lines going in the same direction with a knot here and there

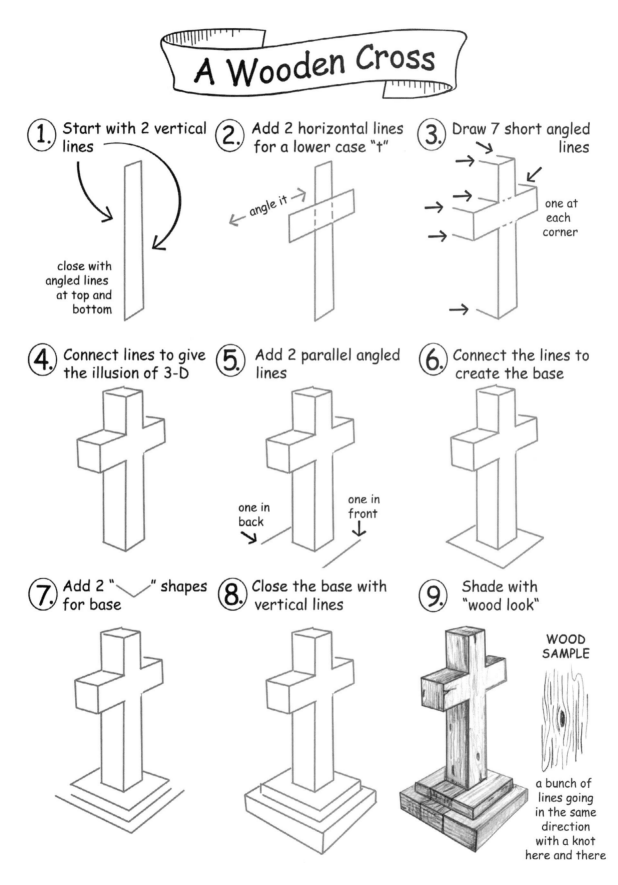

WATER PUDDLE

KNOW:
Organic Shape, Reflection, Depth

UNDERSTAND:
How to create the appearance of depth when drawing organic forms

DO:
Create an original water puddle showing depth, thickness, and reflective properties using the tips provided. Shade. Don't forget the water droplets!

VOCABULARY:
Depth - The apparent distance from front to back or near to far in an artwork. When depth refers to an object's smallest dimension, then this distance can also be called its thickness.

Organic - An irregular shape that might be found in nature, rather than a regular, mechanical shape

Reflection - An image given back by a reflecting surface, such as that of a mirror or still waters

Water Puddles

1. Start with an organic shape

2. Add a "thickness" that follows the contour of the shape on one side.

3. Shade the rim you just created

Leave some white spots for "highlights"

4. Add some random oval droplets

5. Lightly shade the rounded edges on the "top" of the puddle

You can use this same technique when drawing puzzle pieces, too!

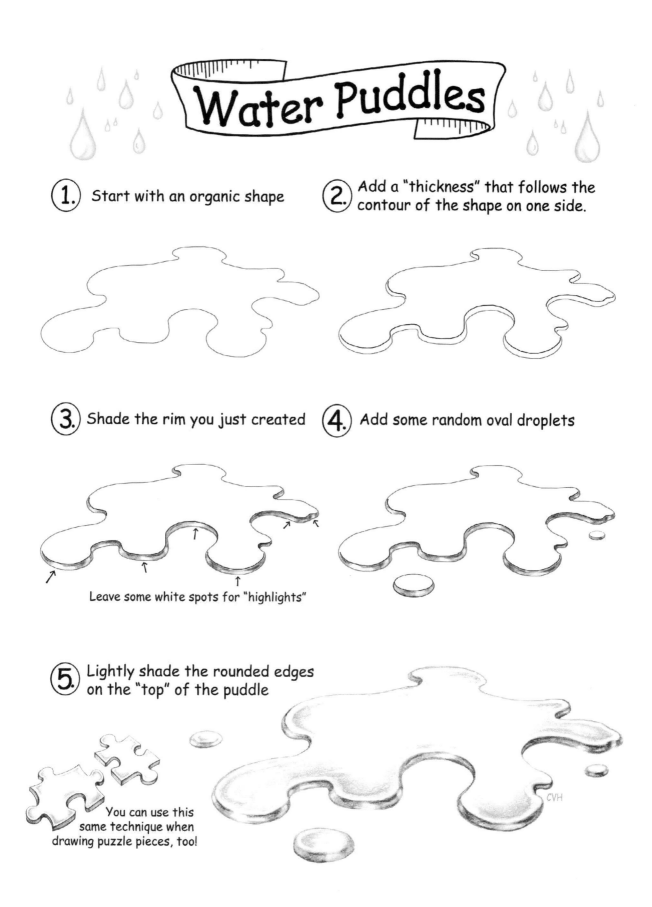

CVH

WATER PUDDLE FLOATERS

KNOW:
• Basic shape construction in drawing
• Shape and form are two of the seven elements of art

UNDERSTAND:
• The difference between shape and form
• Volume
• Shading
• Layering/Overlapping

DO:
Use the knowledge learned in the "Water Puddles" drawing project to create a puddle. Choose an item from the "Water Puddle Floaters" sheet (or choose your own) that will "float" on your puddle. Don't forget to shade your object, erase portions of the puddle to indicate reflective qualities and add water rings to show motion!

VOCABULARY:
Form - A three-dimensional shape (height, width, and depth) that encloses volume
Reflection - An image given back by a reflecting surface, such as that of a mirror or still waters
Shape - An enclosed space
Volume - The space within a form

Water Puddle Floaters

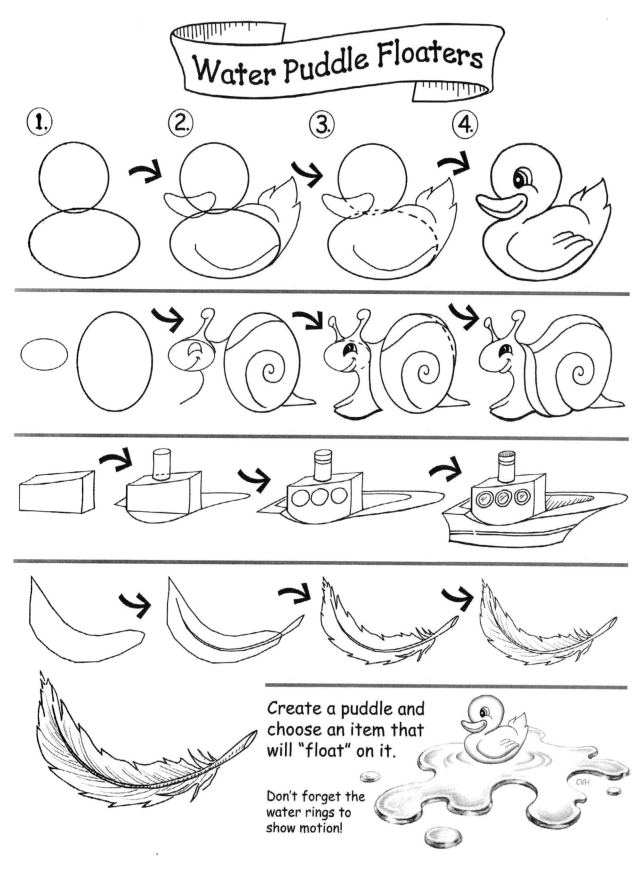

1.
2.
3.
4.

Create a puddle and choose an item that will "float" on it.

Don't forget the water rings to show motion!

CVH

FOOTPRINTS

KNOW:
Simple tips and tricks to make a "mini footprint"

UNDERSTAND:
You can use everyday objects to make prints from and to create designs and patterns

DO:
Follow the steps provided to create a "mini-footprint" design. Try to create both the left and right foot and place them in a staggered pattern so they represent a realistic footprint.

VOCABULARY:
Footprint - The impressions or images left behind by a person walking or running
Pattern - The repetition of any thing including shapes, lines, or colors
Print - A shape or mark made from a block, plate or other object that is covered with wet color (usually ink or paint) and then pressed onto a flat surface
Repetition - A way of combining elements of art so that the same elements are used over and over again. Thus, a certain color or shape might be used several times in the same picture.
Stagger - To arrange unevenly or in a various zigzag or overlapping position

This may take a little practice to get it right but it's a fun and interesting way to make a "footprint"

Footprints

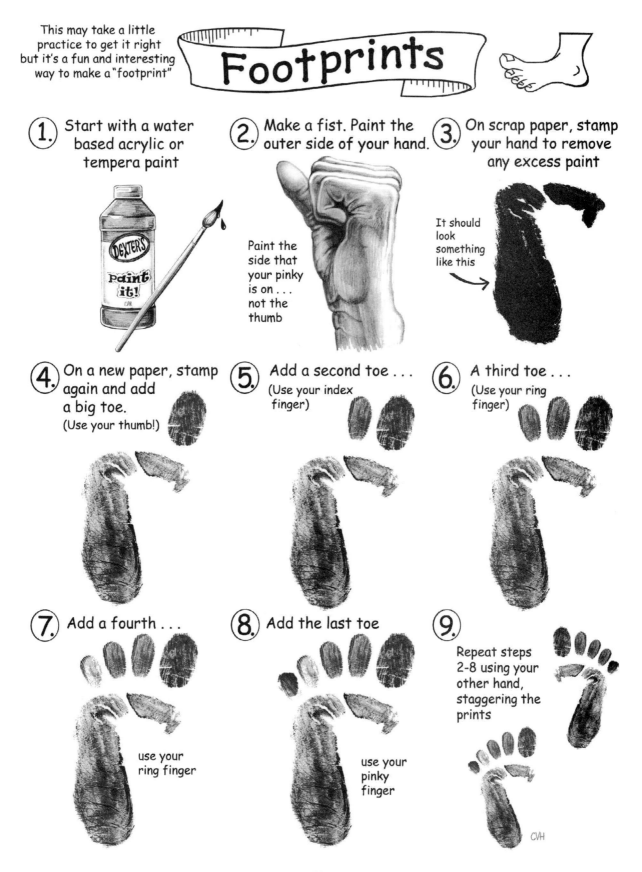

1. Start with a water based acrylic or tempera paint

2. Make a fist. Paint the outer side of your hand.

Paint the side that your pinky is on . . . not the thumb

3. On scrap paper, stamp your hand to remove any excess paint

It should look something like this

4. On a new paper, stamp again and add a big toe.
(Use your thumb!)

5. Add a second toe . . .
(Use your index finger)

6. A third toe . . .
(Use your ring finger)

7. Add a fourth . . .

use your ring finger

8. Add the last toe

use your pinky finger

9. Repeat steps 2-8 using your other hand, staggering the prints

HOW TO DRAW FIRE

KNOW:
Random Lines, Overlapping, Highlight, Value

UNDERSTAND:
• Layering simple shapes helps to show depth and create form
• Varying the value of tones when shading can help to create interest and realism

DO:
• Follow the steps provided to create your own depiction of a fire
• Use value to indicate areas of darkness and lightness
• Erase some areas to create highlights

VOCABULARY:
Highlight - The area on any surface which reflects the most light; to direct attention to or emphasize an area of a drawing through use of value
Overlapping - When one thing lies over another, partly covering it
Random Lines - Haphazard or by chance, to have no pattern
Value - The lightness or darkness of a color or tone

How to Draw Fire

1. Start with a tear drop shape

2. Draw random curvy lines inside

   erase dotted areas

3. Add lines in dotted areas to "thicken" the flames

4. Add a few more random, curvy flames

5. Lightly shade entire flame, partially erasing the center lines

6. Shade

   add small, separate flames

   erase some areas to highlight them

   darken tips

   darken base

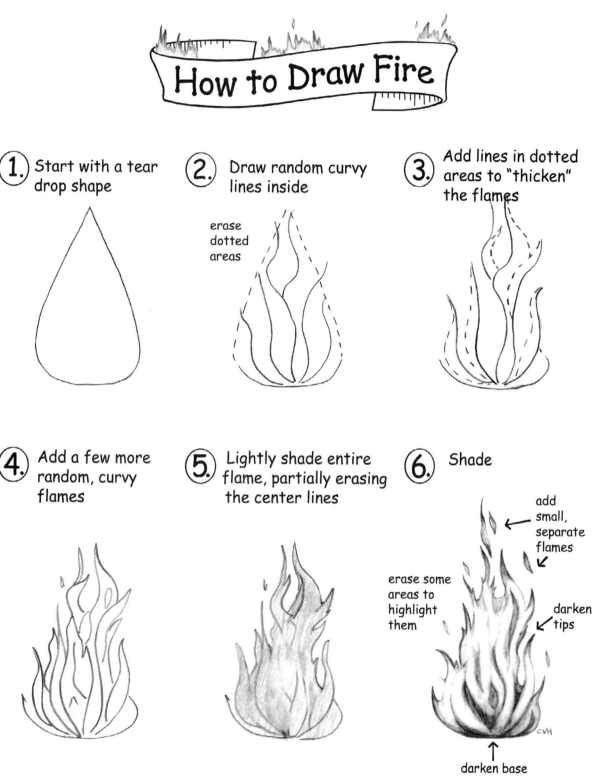

223

HOW TO DRAW A CANDLE

KNOW:
Cylinder, Highlight, Value

UNDERSTAND:
• Cylinders in art give the appearance of a 3D circular tube
• Varying the value of tones when shading can help to create interest and realism

DO:
• Follow the steps provided to create your own depiction of a burning candle
• Use value to indicate areas of darkness and lightness
• Erase some areas to create highlights (more nearest the flame)

VOCABULARY:
Cylinder - A tube that appears three dimensional
Highlight - The area on any surface which reflects the most light; to direct attention to or emphasize an area of a drawing through use of value
Value - The lightness or darkness of a color or tone

Draw a Candle

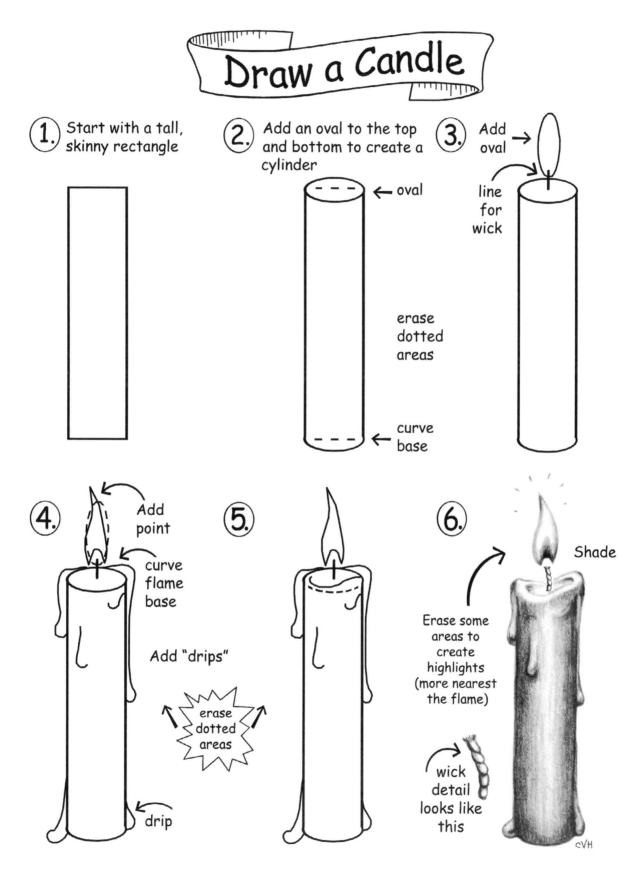

1. Start with a tall, skinny rectangle

2. Add an oval to the top and bottom to create a cylinder

← oval

erase dotted areas

← curve base

3. Add oval →

line for wick

4. Add point

curve flame base

Add "drips"

erase dotted areas

← drip

5. erase dotted areas

6. Shade

Erase some areas to create highlights (more nearest the flame)

wick detail looks like this

cVH

SKULL WITH FLAMES

KNOW:
Exaggerating Features, Highlight, Value

UNDERSTAND:
Use of exaggeration and distortion in an artwork to create a particular style

DO:
• Create your own version of a stylized skull with flames using the guidelines provided OR Practice drawing a generic human skull and exaggerating the features
• Add "extra's" and shade
• Erase some areas to highlight flames

VOCABULARY:
Distortion - To change the way something looks, sometimes deforming or stretching an object
Exaggerate - Overstate, embellish; enlarge or shrink in size
Highlight - The area on any surface which reflects the most light; to direct attention to or emphasize an area of a drawing through use of value

Skull with Flames

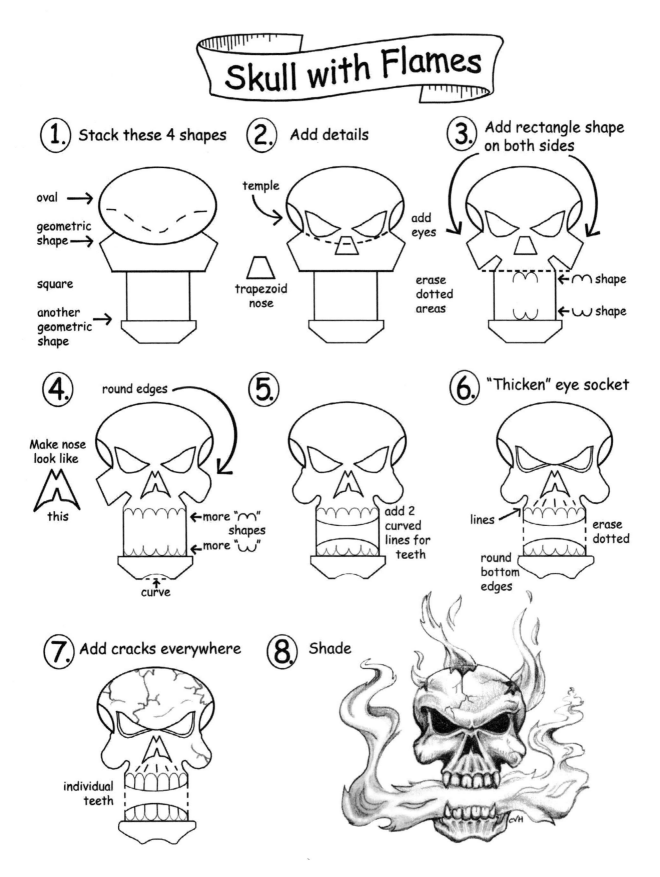

1. Stack these 4 shapes

oval →
geometric shape →
square
another geometric shape →

2. Add details

temple
add eyes
trapezoid nose

3. Add rectangle shape on both sides

erase dotted areas
← ∩ shape
← ⊔ shape

4. round edges

Make nose look like ⋀ this

←more "∩" shapes
←more "⊔"
curve

5.

add 2 curved lines for teeth

6. "Thicken" eye socket

lines →
erase dotted
round bottom edges

7. Add cracks everywhere

individual teeth

8. Shade

227

DRAW SPORTS BALLS

KNOW:
The simple steps to create a variety of sports balls

UNDERSTAND:
• Small changes/additions to basic shapes can help to create specific recognizable images
• The difference between shape and form
• Shading and patterns can help turn shapes into forms

DO:
Follow the steps provided to create at least two of the four sport tools illustrated. Shade.

VOCABULARY:
Form - A three-dimensional shape (height, width, and depth) that encloses volume
Shape - An enclosed space
Volume - Refers to the space within a form

Draw Sports Balls

"BOING"

1. BASKETBALL
Draw a circle

2. Add a slightly curved diagonal

3. Add 3 curves as seen below

4. Shade

CVH

1. FOOTBALL
Start with oval

add curved diagonal

2. Add rounded stripes at ends

3. Add "H" shapes for laces

4. Shade

CVH

1. BASEBALL
Start with circle

2. Add 2 light lines curving in center

3. Add open "V" for stitch detail

4. Shade

CVH

1. HOCKEY PUCK
Start with oval

2. Draw 2 parallel lines on sides

3. Round base to connect

4. Shade

CVH

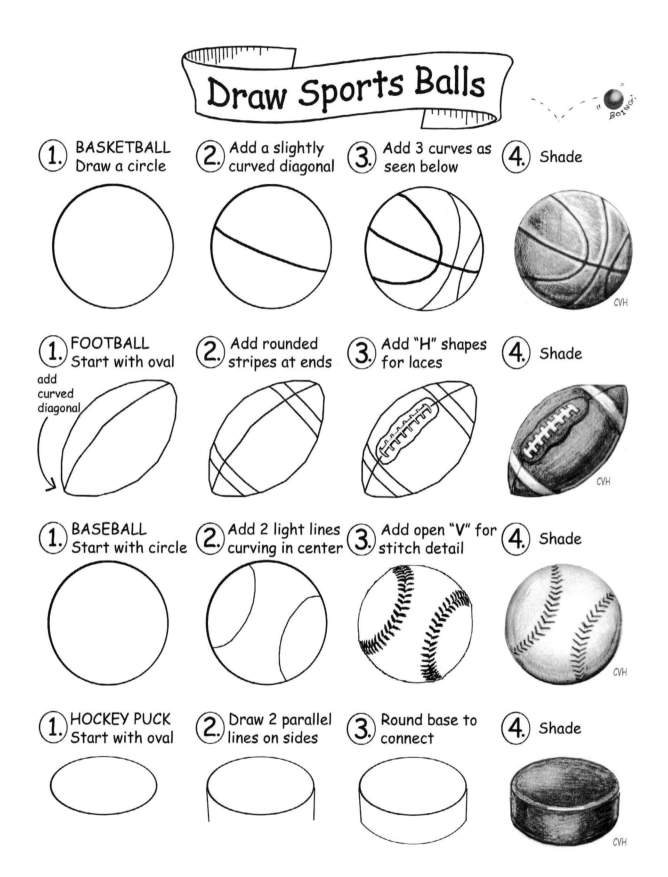

BASKETBALL HOOP

KNOW:
• Simple shapes combined together can create more complex objects
• Overlapping

UNDERSTAND:
• Overlapping and layering items help to create a sense of realism
• Differences in the size of object parts can help to achieve the illusion of depth

DO:
Create an original artwork of your version of a basketball hoop following the steps provided. Try the easy one first, then more difficult version. Don't trace. Shade.

VOCABULARY:
Overlap - When one thing lies over and partly covers something else
Perspective - The technique used to create the illusion of 3D onto a 2D surface. Perspective helps to create a sense of depth or receding space.

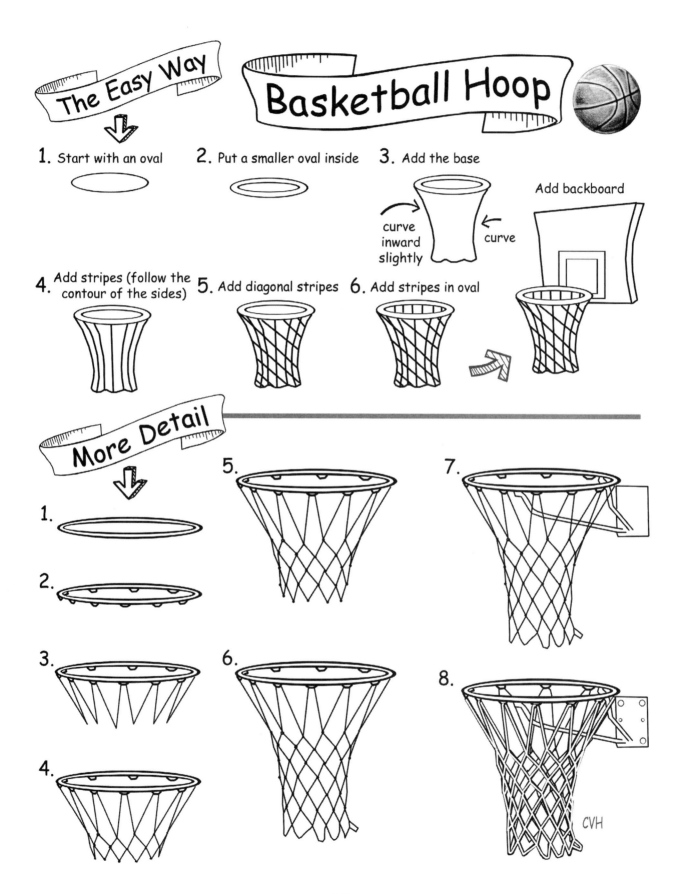

The Easy Way

Basketball Hoop

1. Start with an oval

2. Put a smaller oval inside

3. Add the base
curve inward slightly
curve

Add backboard

4. Add stripes (follow the contour of the sides)

5. Add diagonal stripes

6. Add stripes in oval

More Detail

1.

2.

3.

4.

5.

6.

7.

8.

CVH

231

DRAW A BARE TREE

KNOW:
• A basic tree shape can be simplified as a cylinder
• Asymmetry
• The 'Y' Trick (branches look like the letter Y)

UNDERSTAND:
• Cylinders in art give the appearance of a 3D circular tube
• Branches grow up and out on most trees (not down)
• Every tree is unique - no two are exactly alike
• Trees may be similar on both sides but not symmetrical

DO:
• Create your own tree using 'The "Y" Trick" technique
• Shade

VOCABULARY:
Asymmetry - The parts of a design are organized so that one side differs from the other
Cylinder - A tube that appears three dimensional

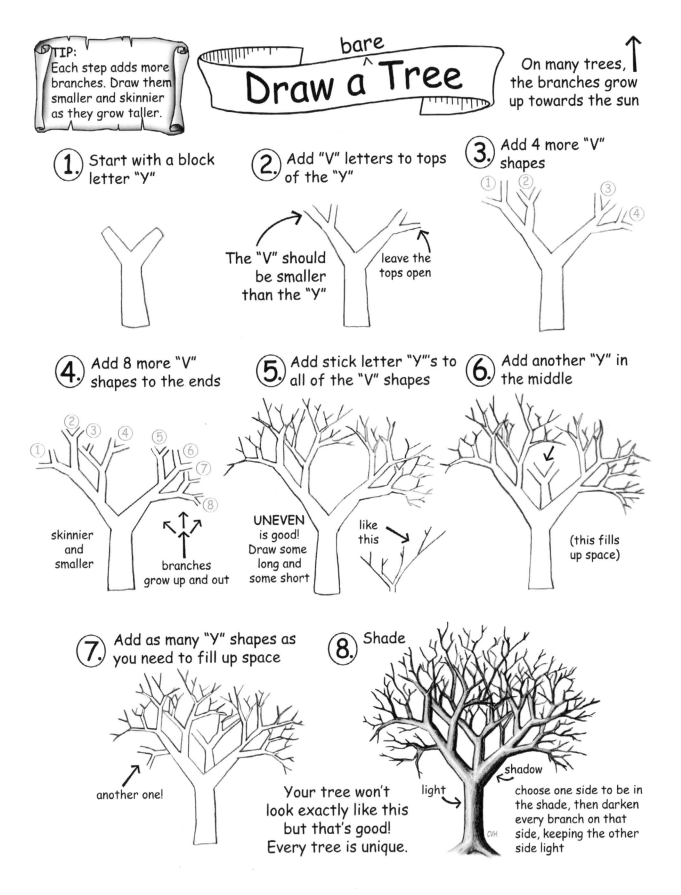

TIP: Each step adds more branches. Draw them smaller and skinnier as they grow taller.

Draw a bare Tree

On many trees, the branches grow up towards the sun

1. Start with a block letter "Y"

2. Add "V" letters to tops of the "Y"

The "V" should be smaller than the "Y"

leave the tops open

3. Add 4 more "V" shapes

4. Add 8 more "V" shapes to the ends

skinnier and smaller

branches grow up and out

5. Add stick letter "Y"'s to all of the "V" shapes

UNEVEN is good! Draw some long and some short

like this

6. Add another "Y" in the middle

(this fills up space)

7. Add as many "Y" shapes as you need to fill up space

another one!

Your tree won't look exactly like this but that's good! Every tree is unique.

8. Shade

light

shadow

choose one side to be in the shade, then darken every branch on that side, keeping the other side light

CVH

DRAW A PALM TREE

KNOW:
• A basic tree shape can be simplified as a cylinder
• Asymmetry

UNDERSTAND:
• Simplifying an artwork consists of breaking down the major parts of an object into simple shapes
• Every tree is unique - no two are exactly alike
• Trees are asymmetrical

DO:
• Follow the steps provided to create a detailed palm tree that starts from simple lines
• Use a cylinder trunk to convey the illusion of depth. Students will also consider size, position, detail and shading.

VOCABULARY:
Asymmetry - The parts of a design are organized so that one side differs from the other
Cylinder - A tube that appears three dimensional

Draw a Palm Tree

ALOHA!

1. Start with a curved trunk

2. Add "spider" legs on top

3. Add rounded lines to trunk

grass sprout

4. One at a time, add lines to each "spider" leg for leaves

5. Do this for each "spider" leg

(notice how lines are longer in the center)

6. Add more leaves at top of trunk

7. Add a smaller tree bending the opposite way

use dots to create "sand"

CVH

GRAFFITI ART

KNOW:
• Graffiti Art and rap music became popular in the early 1970's when art and music classes were cut from NY schools and students needed an outlet for their creativity.
• Texture

UNDERSTAND:
• The need for artistic expression
• Textures can be visually created with line and shadow

DO:
• Create a textured brick wall using learned techniques
• Choose or create a font and/or design to place on your wall. Be sure to add shadows.

VOCABULARY:
Artistic Expression - To express oneself through visual art creations, songs, poetry, etc. The emotions of an artist communicated through color, subject matter and style
Font - A complete set of characters and spacing of one size of type
Texture - The way something looks like it might feel like in an artwork

Graffiti Art

1. Start with 2 long rectangles

2. Center a 3rd brick underneath

3. Add another (stagger them)

4. Keep adding bricks until you have a complete wall

TIP: You can use a ruler to evenly space the bricks then erase lines in between, BUT, it looks more authentic if the bricks are not perfect rectangles

erase

"thicken" bottom and left edges

lightly shade leaving a thin, white edge

smudge with finger

5. NEXT STEP...

Choose your *lettering*

● Draw your word in thick letters on top of the bricks

● Erase inside the letters a little (you still want some brick to show through)

● Add some "drips" to the base of each letter

BLOCK
BUBBLE
Cursive
old english

Choose one of these or make up your own lettering style

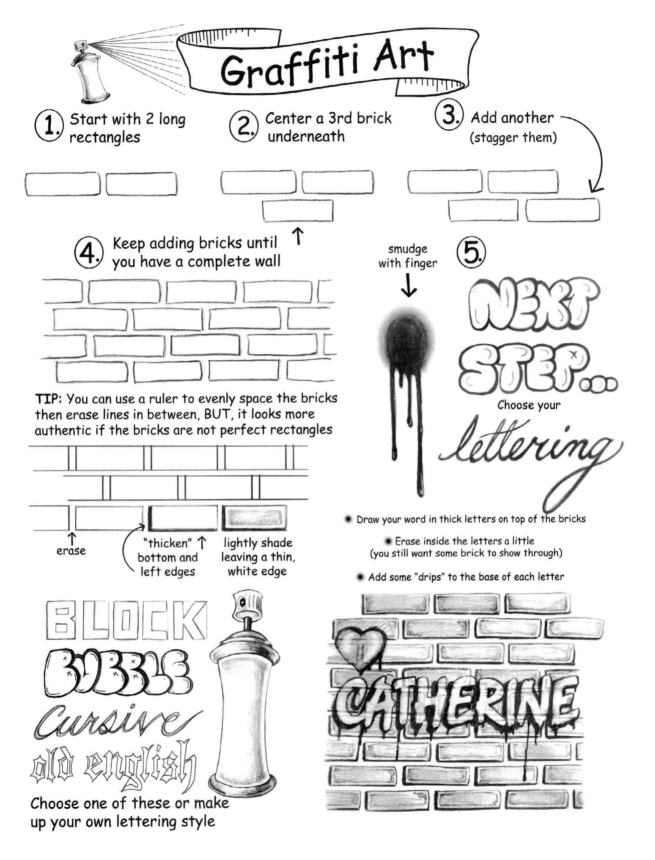

COOL LETTERING STYLES

KNOW:
• Font, Typeface, Lettering

UNDERSTAND:
"Type" is a letterform produced electronically or photographically, most often with a computer. Before computers took over this function in the late twentieth century, type was a small block of metal or wood bearing a raised letter or character on the upper end that leaves a printed impression when inked and pressed on paper.

DO:
• Create your own typeface or choose a style seen on the handout
• Spelling your name or complete the alphabet with your font. Be sure to add detail, thickness or shading

VOCABULARY:
Font - A complete set of characters and spacing of one size of type
Typeface - A full set of letterforms, numerals, punctuations and other characters unified by consistent visual qualities (also known as font)

Cool Lettering Styles

Block Letters: Make a box, carve out the letter inside with straight lines (no curves), then erase the parts of the box not used for the letter.

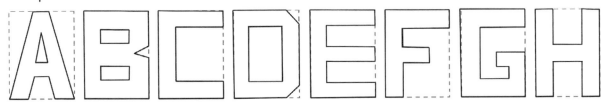

Bubble Letters: Take the block letter and "blow it up" so there are no straight lines. It becomes a balloon!

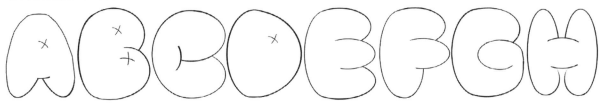

Shadow Lettering: The letter appears through the shaadowed 3-D edge - not the actual letter

Fancy: Make one side of the letter thinner than the other. Put a curly-q at the end.

Tips for creating graffiti:
Overlap your letters, create an interesting pattern inside them, stagger them (have some letters slightly lower on page) and make a shadow!

HOMEBOY SKULL

KNOW:
Exaggerating Features, Distortion, Value

UNDERSTAND:
Use of exaggeration and distortion in an artwork to create a particular style

DO:
• Create your own version of a stylized skull with a hat using the guidelines provided OR Practice drawing a generic human skull and exaggerating the features
• Add "extra's" and shade
• Erase some areas to indicate highlights

VOCABULARY:
Distortion - To change the way something looks — sometimes deforming or stretching an object
Exaggerate - Overstate, embellish; enlarge or shrink in size
Highlight - The area on any surface which reflects the most light; to direct attention to or emphasize an area of a drawing through use of value

Homeboy Skull

1. Draw 1 big and 2 small circles
2. Add a rectangle
3. Add chin and jaw lines
4. Add nose and hat line
5. Add eye area details

6. Add 4 teeth
7. 4 more teeth, hat tab & nose
8. 4 more teeth & rim eyes — erase
9. 4 more teeth & thicken tab
10. 4 more teeth & mouth lines

11. Add a tilted square
12. Round into hat
13. Add snaps & tooth lines
14. Eye line detail
15. Hat line detail

16. Add hat brim
17. Random cracks
18. Shade

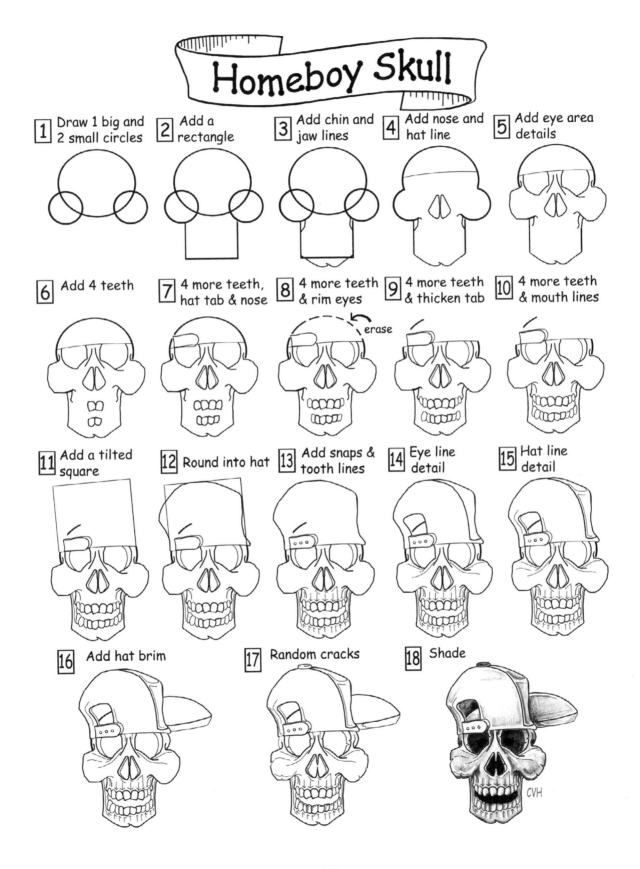

CVH

BACK OF THE HAND

KNOW:
• Creating a likeness from observation
• Many objects (man made and natural) are based on the cylinder

UNDERSTAND:
Shading using value scale tones will achieve a more realistic rendering

DO:
• Practice drawing your hand using the proposed techniques
• Make the darkest values between the fingers and knuckle creases. Erase some spots on the knuckle, center finger and center hand to create a natural highlight effect.

VOCABULARY:
Cylinder - A tube that appears three dimensional
Highlight - The area on any surface which reflects the most light; to direct attention to or emphasize an area of a drawing through use of value

1.

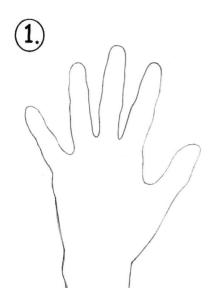

Start by tracing your hand.
If you are right handed,
trace your left, etc.
TIP: To get the best hand shape,
keep your pencil at a 90°angle.

2.

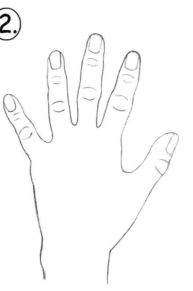

Next, add fingernails and a
⌒ shape for each knuckle.
NOTE: There are 2 knuckle joints
in the actual finger

3.

Look at your hand.
Do you see skin above the nails?
Do you have white tips on your nails?
Can you see the fine hand bones?
Do you have many knuckle lines?
If so - add them.

4.

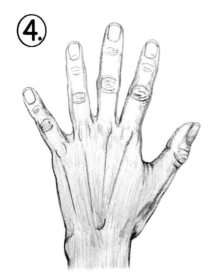

Lightly shade the entire
hand gray. Darken the outline
of the hand edges and the
knuckles.

5.

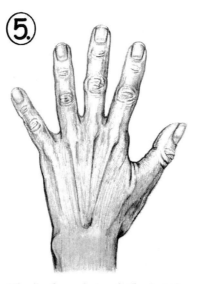

Shade the edges of the hand
and each finger. Look at your
real hand and notice the dark
and light areas. Deepen the
darker areas.

6.

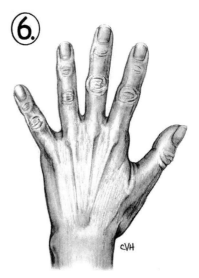

Add the finishing touches.
Use your eraser to lighten the
knuckles and the center of
the fingers.

PALM OF THE HAND

KNOW:
• Creating a likeness from observation
• Many objects (man made and natural) are based on the cylinder

UNDERSTAND:
Shading using value scale tones will achieve a more realistic rendering

DO:
• Practice drawing your hand using the proposed techniques
• Make the darkest values between the fingers and knuckle creases. Erase some spots on the finger pads and between the creases to create a natural highlight effect.

VOCABULARY:
Cylinder - A tube that appears three dimensional
Highlight - The area on any surface which reflects the most light; to direct attention to or emphasize an area of a drawing through use of value

Palm of the Hand

1.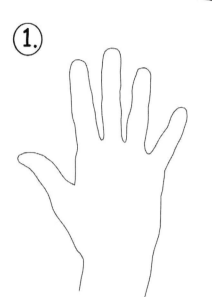

Start by tracing your hand - palm up.

TIP: To get the best hand shape, keep your pencil at a 90°angle.

2.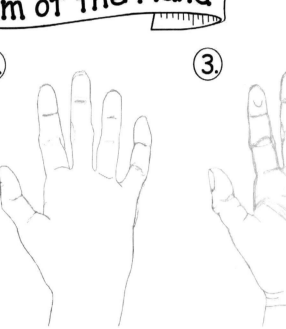

Relax your hand. The fingers will curl in a bit. Lightly sketch the changes in the finger angles.

3.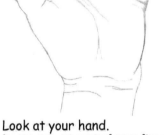

Look at your hand.
Do you see any part of your fingernail? Everyone has a different line pattern in their palm. Draw yours.

4.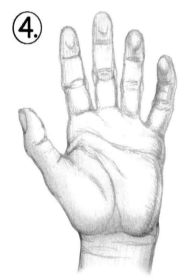

Lightly shade the entire hand gray. Darken the outline of the hand edges and the knuckle creases.

5.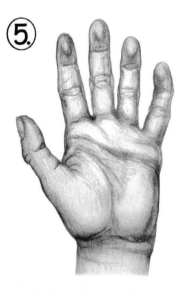

Shade the edges of the hand and each finger. Look at your real hand and notice the dark and light areas. Deepen the darker areas.

6.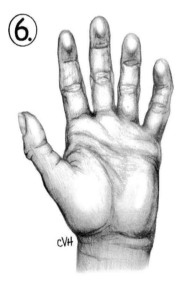

Add the finishing touches. Use your eraser to lighten the palm, between the creases and the pads of the fingers.

COMEDY & TRAGEDY MASKS

KNOW:
• Expression
• Origins of the Comedy/Tragedy Masks

UNDERSTAND:
• These masks originated in Ancient Greece
• Masks have played an important role in the history of drama
• The current symbol for theater
• Expression is a non-verbal behavior that communicates emotion or a movement of the face that conveys an emotional state

DO:
Create an original Comedy/Tragedy mask drawing that shows expression using the steps provided

VOCABULARY:
Comedy - Funny entertainment

Mask - A face covering. Usually it is something worn on the face, with openings for the eyes, to conceal one's identity, either for partying (as at a masquerade ball), to frighten or amuse (as at Halloween), for ritual, or for performance as by actors in Greek, Roman, and Japanese theater.

Tragedy - Drama

Comedy & Tragedy Masks

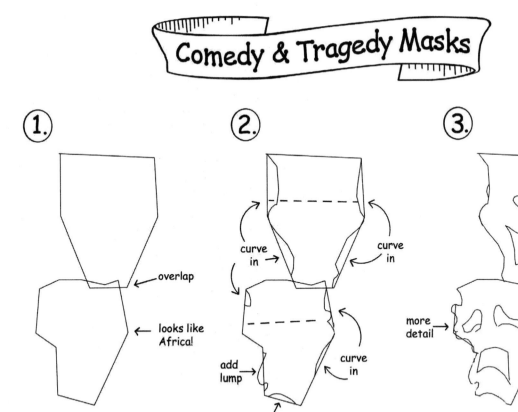

1.

Start by blocking off the basic mask shape. Draw lightly as you will be erasing these guides in step 3.

overlap

looks like Africa!

2.

"Carve out" the details. Add guide lines for eyes.

curve in → *curve in*
add lump → *curve in*

3.

Erase original guidelines. Add eyes, nose and mouth.

more detail →

4.

Add brows, lips and "thickness" to the eyes.

5.

Add design lines.

6.

Shade. Add banner with text if desired.

Laugh Now... ...Cry Later

STACKS OF CASH

KNOW:
Adding pattern and shading to an object give it form and dimension

UNDERSTAND:
• Using the principles of a cube to create a 3D rectangle
• The use of receding lines to show perspective

DO:
Create an original artwork of a "Stacks of Cash" that demonstrate perspective. Add at least 3 stacks and lots of "extra's". Don't forget shadows!

VOCABULARY:
Cube - A polyhedron having six square faces; a square that appears 3D
Perspective - The point from which an object or scene is viewed
Receding Lines - Lines that move back or away from the foreground

Stacks of Cash

1.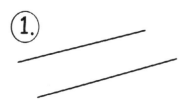

Start with 2 parallel lines angled downward

2.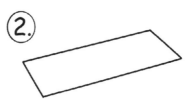

Connect on the sides to create a slanted rectangle

3.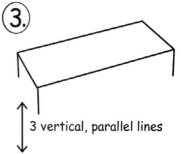

3 vertical, parallel lines

4.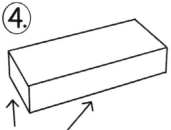

Connect with 2 angled lines

5.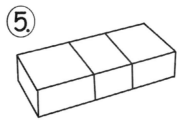

"Wrap" the 3-D rectangle in the center

6.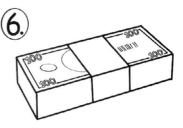

Add design details

7.

Add random parallel dashed lines to show lots of stacked bills

8.

Add as many stacks as you want. Shade.

EASY SPIDER WEB

KNOW:
Symmetry, Asymmetry, Radial Balance

UNDERSTAND:
A spider web is based on a circle with its design extending from or focused upon its center

DO:
• Create an original spider web design based on radial balance
• Add a spider and other "extra's"

VOCABULARY:
Symmetry - (or symmetrical balance) - The parts of an image or object organized so that one side duplicates, or mirrors, the other
Symmetry is among the ten classes of patterns
Radial or Rotational Balance is any type of balance based on a circle with its design extending from or focused upon its center

Easy Spider Web

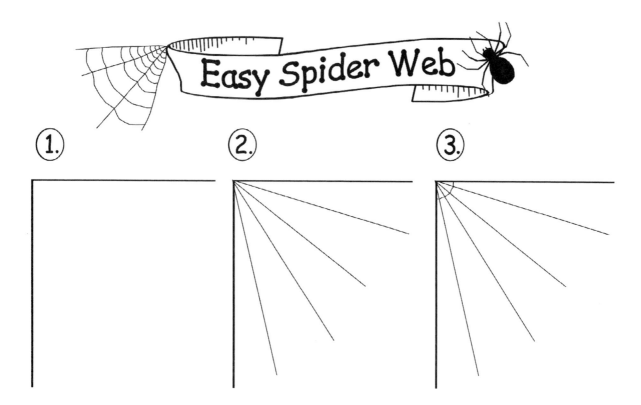

1.
Start with a 90 degree angle. This will be the corner the spider web will be "spun" in.

2.
Draw 4 or 5 equally spaced lines radiating from the corner. (Like spokes of a bicycle wheel)

3.
Create a layer of lines that curve around the upper corner. They should look like upside-down waves

4.
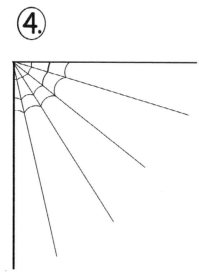

Add a few more layers of the web.

5.

Continue to add web lines, each layer further apart from the last.

6.

Finish the web.
Add a dangling spider.
Remember: Spiders have 8 legs!